A Powerful Book on the Subject of Control

This is one of the most powerful books I have ever read on the subject of control. The candor with which Lisa writes causes you not only to relate on a personal level, but also to take a swift inventory within.

In this book Lisa reveals that those who seek to control their lives are in bondage and lack the very freedom and control they seek. However, those who have allowed God to take the reins of their lives are in control and walk in the liberty of life in Christ Jesus.

Marilyn Hickey
Marilyn Hickey Ministries

An Example of an Open Heart

I find it amazing that a woman of God would tell us she wanted to slam her son into the wall. I'm amazed that she would announce to a group of hungry women that she was a mess. Anger hides behind many excuses, but Lisa hides behind none of them. Next to the Bible this book is perhaps the most important book a woman will ever read about finding her true self and her true value to the kingdom of God.

Have the courage to read it with an open heart. I believe it could change your life forever.

Lindsay Roberts
Oral Roberts Ministries
Tulsa, Oklahoma

Jesus Is the Answer

I am blessed to read a book that brings Christians back to the fact that Jesus wants not only to be our Savior, Healer, Deliverer and Restorer, but also our Lord. Only through daily submitting our wills to Him will we be truly fulfilled and at peace within ourselves and with others.

Many Christian homes have been destroyed because of selfishness and pride. The world is looking for those who not only speak "Jesus is the Answer" but also live "Jesus is the Answer." I commend Lisa for taking the time to write and share her own life experiences to help others.

Sharon Daugherty
Victory Christian Center
Tulsa, Oklahoma

Help for Every Reader

Lisa, my brave friend, has written a very poignant and relevant book. Realizing there are times when we all must deal with problem areas in our lives, this extremely honest book can help every reader, male or female. Thank you, Lisa, for allowing us to see a real person still being transformed.

Mary Brown
Music That Ministers

Recommended to Every Child of God

Lisa Bevere's book, *Out of Control and Loving It!* is a practical, transparent and openly honest account of the emotions we all face on a daily basis. I find this book refreshing and one that I can honestly recommend to every child of God. Read this book. You'll not be sorry.

Paula White
Co-pastor of South Tampa Christian Center

Maximize Your Potential

Realness is bringing a freshness to the body of Christ in this critical hour. Lisa's transparency is a testimony of her deliverance and spiritual maturity. If your heart's desire is to maximize your potential, it will trigger you to face the truth and allow that truth to transform your life as well. As Lisa has learned, we all must exchange our control for His Christ-like nature.

Our insecurities and lack of knowing who we are force us to crave to control circumstances, situations and even other people. As Lisa so clearly admits, when we are not submitted to the authority of the Holy Spirit, control controls us. Control is crippling us. Exchange it for His character.

Gina Pearson
Higher Dimensions Family Church
Tulsa, Oklahoma

Refreshing Truth That Will Help Others

How refreshing to find someone so honest, selfless, forthright and transparent as Lisa Bevere evidences in her book, *Out of Control and Loving It!* It is indeed the truth that sets, makes and keeps us free. Lisa evidences in her book that she has found His freedom and shares it in truth that will help others to break out of control and love it.

Dr. Fuchsia Pickett
Fuchsia Pickett Ministries

Freedom From Satanic Snares

I come from an abusive background and was nearly thirty years old before I let God heal me, which just demonstrates how Satan wants to keep us locked up in a prison of secrets, hidden sins and unforgiveness. Lisa has severed the tie of unforgiveness, blown open the door of hidden sins and showed a perfect escape route from the demonic prison of secrets.

God wants all things out of the darkness and into the light. Lisa will show you how to get there — to freedom, forgiveness and godly joy. Every person I know, including myself, will benefit from this book. You can be free from all satanic snares, including anger, strife and unforgiveness.

Lisa, you heard God, you obeyed and you wrote. Thank you.

Cheryl Salem
Miss America 1980

Lisa Bevere

Out of Control and Loving It!

Charisma
HOUSE
A STRANG COMPANY

OUT OF CONTROL AND LOVING IT! by Lisa Bevere
Published by Charisma House
A Strang Company
600 Rinehart Road
Lake Mary, FL 32746
www.charismahouse.com

Unless otherwise noted, all Scripture quotations are from the
Holy Bible, New International Version. Copyright © 1973,
1978, 1984, International Bible Society. Used by permission.

Scripture quotations marked NKJV are from the New King
James Version of the Bible. Copyright © 1979, 1980, 1982 by
Thomas Nelson, Inc., publishers. Used by permission.

Scripture quotations marked AMP are from the Amplified Bible.
Old Testament copyright © 1965, 1987 by the Zondervan
Corporation. The Amplified New Testament copyright © 1954,
1958, 1987 by the Lockman Foundation. Used by permission.

Library of Congress Catalog Card Number: 96-83756
International Standard Book Number: 0-88419-436-1

05 06 07 08 — 18 17 16 15
Printed in the United States of America

ACKNOWLEDGMENTS

My deepest appreciation to my husband, John, who believed enough in me never to allow me to remain comfortable but who has always challenged me to move into the realm of God's grace and call on my life. May we never be satisfied until we behold His glory. You are truly God's gracious gift, my friend and closest confidant.

To my four precious sons. Addison, your tenderness, determination and zeal for righteousness is commendable. Austin, your creativity, sensitivity and courage is inspirational. Alexander, your love, joy and laughter is delightful. Arden, your strength and fiery determination challenges me to live life to its fullest. Boys, I will always love you deeply. Each of you is a unique and special blessing from God.

To my mother, whose encouragement throughout this project meant so much to me. The best is yet to be.

To our entire staff at John Bevere Ministries. May God reward your faithful diligence.

To the Creation House staff who labored along with us. Deborah, you have been so supportive throughout the editing process. Steve and Joy, we consider you partners and friends to this ministry.

To my Father God. You more than anyone else know how utterly impossible this book would have been without Your direction and guidance. I fall upon Your grace, eternally grateful.

CONTENTS

Foreword
by John Bevere

We live in a world where lawlessness abounds. Today more than 65 percent of our population has been marred by the tragedy of divorce. This is often the end result of wounding words and actions. In our day many have been abused, both verbally and physically. What makes it worse is that the abuse occurs most often at the hands of the very people who are expected to nourish and protect the ones abused. Even more damaging is the fact that most of the pain is inflicted during childhood when personality and views on life are being developed.

No one has escaped the abundance of hatred, jealousy, greed and selfishness that has spawned breaches and betrayals in relationships within our society. All of this and much more is contributing to a major problem called "lack of trust."

In light of this, most would never confess a love for being

out of control. Rather, most would say, "Out of control and despising it is the way I feel." Because of this lack of trust in today's world, most strive to take control of their lives and their surroundings, thinking it's the only way to survive. People believe that to be in control means they will be secure and successful. In these times, men, and especially women, are taught either directly or indirectly to be independent and self-sustaining. They learn how to control.

In this book Lisa shows that those who control their lives, relationships and surroundings are the ones who are in bondage. The very freedom they seek is lost. Conversely, those who have relinquished control to the Lord are the ones who are actually in control and walk in life and freedom.

Jesus said, "For whoever desires to save [or control] his life will lose it, but whoever loses [control of] his life for My sake will find it" (Matt. 16:25, NKJV). These are easy words to recite, but they are hard words to live, especially in a society where selfishness abounds.

This book revolves around these words of Jesus. It is a very practical book that will show how to relinquish control to our Savior and find the peace so many are looking for. The revelation knowledge contained in this book is both profound and life-changing. When I read the chapters, I exclaimed, "Not only should women read this book, but men also." I can see that many couples are going to read it together.

Being married to Lisa, I can honestly say the truths you are about to experience in this book are not just a studied-out teaching. I have walked with her through every one of them. I have been able to witness the transforming work of the Holy Spirit in her life. She has grown rapidly in the Lord because of her willingness to be open and honest about herself in the time of the Lord's training. Her example has encouraged me to be open and honest about my own life as well. As you read you will not be afraid to open the guarded areas of your own life to the One who loves you.

There is no other person I respect and love more than Lisa. I trust her with my life, not just because she's my wife and best friend, but because she is a woman who truly fears the Lord.

Thank you, Lisa, for being the godly wife and mother you are. Thank you for obeying the Master and bringing forth this message of His. I am grateful to the Lord for the privilege of being married to you.

John Bevere
Author and speaker
John Bevere Ministries

Foreword
by Suzanne Hinn

The Lord is shaking everything that can be shaken, and only those with their feet firmly planted on Christ will be able to stand in the days ahead. Those with godly character and integrity and those who walk before Him in holiness will dare to say, "I'm living out of control and loving it."

Lisa Bevere is a woman I greatly admire and respect. She and her husband came to be part of the ministry team at World Outreach Center, pastored by my husband, Benny Hinn, as youth ministers. After a short season the Lord launched them into their new evangelistic ministries.

Lisa demonstrates a humble spirit in which character and integrity are a part of her daily walk. Her life portrays a deep inner strength in her calling as a wife, mother, friend and inspirational speaker. Her ability to walk in truth and obedience has developed sensitivity to hearing and responding to the voice of God.

In this book, *Out of Control and Loving It!,* she describes what can happen when we become clay in the Potter's hands. She reminds us that we will remain captive to the flesh unless we allow God's Spirit to crucify the flesh. She describes how to take responsibility for our past failures, fears and anger without using them as an excuse for not changing our daily behavior. We must not "excuse it," as she says, instead "crucify it." I agree that our self lives must die daily so the Lord can truly be in control of every area in our lives.

Lisa reveals that only when we are "out of control" do we truly begin to understand our God-given authority. It is then flesh habits and fears can be crucified so that more of Christ and His love is released in us. The world will never see Jesus unless He is seen in us, and we can say with Lisa that because it is God's way we are "loving every moment of it."

When you read Lisa's book you will grow and change because you know she's speaking from her own practical experience. She deals with the secret of applying God's truth to life by the transforming work of the Holy Spirit.

Suzanne Hinn
Orlando, Florida

Introduction

Some of you reading this book may find your lives out of control — and you hate it! Everything around you is chaos. Things are out of control because *you* are in control. God is challenging us to relinquish management of our lives so we can be out of control — and love it.

This book is a record of my personal journey from fearful, fanatical control to a place of rest under God's control. I have been brutally open and honest in the hope that you would see yourself in my fears and foolishness. So, as you read this book, let it reflect on your life and not the life of another.

We are a people in transition. During transition God is more concerned with our condition than our comfort. Because this is true, often He will allow the upheaval of our circumstances, finances, social standing, security and relationships. Seasons of change are crucial, critical times in our lives. It is in the whirlwind of transition and turmoil that we find out what we are made of and who is actually in control.

I found that whenever I was in charge I ended up with a mess. Even though I wanted the mess fixed, I was afraid to let go for fear it would grow bigger. Well, it is time to let go. When God is in control, even our messes are ordered under His care. This is not a book about indifference; it is one about caring and loving enough to turn loose.

You may be lamenting, "I'd let go if only I knew how!" You let go when you make your will subservient to God's will. It is when we lose our lives that He can save them.

We all have areas in our lives where we have relinquished our guardianship. Yet there are other areas we are afraid to entrust even to God's care. God is asking us to yield completely so He can surround us with His protection and care. He wants us "in over our heads."

I like to compare letting go with the process of learning to swim. It can be both exhilarating and terrifying. In order to swim you must first learn to float, allowing the water to hold you up. Only then do you discover the freedom and liberty of swimming. This natural principle reflects a spiritual transition from our natural rule to the rule of the Holy Spirit.

The body of Christ is the collective strength of all of its members. God is in the process of healing each joint and member in His body. To accomplish this He is dealing with us as individuals in order that we might be whole. This book is my testimony of this refinement in my personal life. Though this refining is far from complete, I believe the witness of this process will encourage you to forget what is behind and strain toward what is ahead (Phil. 3:13).

PART I

The Captive Woman

I was tired of acting free
when I was not, tired of acting
strong when I was in fact weak.

1

Awake, Daughter of Zion

A wake, awake, O Zion, clothe yourself with strength. Put on your garments of splendor, O Jerusalem, the holy city. The uncircumcised and defiled will not enter you again. Shake off your dust; rise up, sit enthroned, O Jerusalem. Free yourself from the chains on your neck, O captive Daughter of Zion" (Is. 52:1-2).

I begin with this scripture because I believe hidden within its poignant imagery is a wealth of truth. These truths began an awakening in my life, one which resonated through my soul until my entire being was touched. I share it's precious message of freedom with you. I invite you to ponder and dissect it with me, searching each segment for its hidden truth. Together let's visit this captive daughter of Zion.

I envision her hopelessly chained to a wall of stone. I see the footprints in the dusty earth where she struggled to escape. Her neck is rubbed raw where the metal yoke encircles it. She mindlessly paces the length of her chain, retracing each step, in search of some key to set her free. She scans the dust, poking and probing each crevice in the wall.

Hopeless and discouraged she now sits in the dust, shoulders bent, clothes ragged, strength spent. Though it is day, she lapses into an exhausted stupor of restless sleep.

Then I see a strong messenger arrive. I watch over his shoulder as he pities this worn and wounded woman. He stands before her silently watching as her head tosses in her sleep. Suddenly he steps forward, shakes her and calls her by name.

> Awake, awake, O Zion, clothe yourself with strength. Put on your garments of splendor...Shake off your dust; rise up, sit enthroned, O Jerusalem. Free yourself from the chains on your neck, O captive Daughter of Zion.

She struggles to her feet, swaying weakly and pointing to the wall, the chain and her yoke. "Help me," she pleads as she strains for his hand, but he steps back beyond her reach.

Once again he repeats his message, pauses, turns and walks away.

Bewildered she calls after him, but the wind snatches her voice, and he does not return. She laments, "The wall is too solid; my chain, too heavy; and I, too weak to lift myself out from all this!" In despair she strains at her chain until she no longer can stand the pressure of resisting. She moves back to the shelter of her wall. At least there she can feel what is behind her and see what is in front of her.

I rehearsed this scenario over and over in my mind, acutely feeling her pain and frustration. Why was my vision so clear? Because I too was a captive daughter of Zion.

It is a contradiction for a daughter of Zion to be captive. A daughter is an heir, and a daughter of Zion is an heir of God! How could any child of God be held captive? Yet it was true that I was bound.

I would comfort myself, thinking, *Perhaps if I attend this seminar or if that person prays for me I'll be free.* So with each new teaching or sermon I'd back up then run, endeavoring to break loose, declaring, "This time I've had enough!" But my chain was too strong, and its length always yanked me back to the bitter reality of my bondage.

Tired of constant disappointment I resigned myself to my condition. I decided it was better not to hope than to hope and only be disappointed again. So I concealed my chains and quietly moved within the confines of my restrictions.

Then the Holy Spirit blew the words of Isaiah 52:1-2 my way. They intrigued me with their vivid imagery and contrast. I drew a parallel between this ancient prisoner and myself.

I was tired of acting free when I was not, tired of acting strong when I was in fact weak. I hungered more for freedom than I cared for the approval of those around me. I had already discovered that their approval could never set me free.

So began my quest. No man, woman or ministry could ever set me free. My freedom lay hidden somewhere in this message from my Father, my Maker.

In my mind I visited this captive daughter of Zion many times. Each time she looked a little worse and more hopeless than the last. The last time I saw her she sat numbly in the dust as the messenger spoke to her.

She lifted her head only slightly as she silently watched him walk away. It seemed the sun was setting on her hope for freedom. Who was this messenger? Had her enemy sent him to taunt her with dreams that would never come true?

But this time as the stranger mounted the hill that would

once again take him from her sight he turned and looked back.

Puzzled, she scanned his outline against the setting sun. The wind carried his words to her ears again, "Awake, awake, O Zion..."

But this time the voice was different. She recognized who was calling her. It was the voice of one she loved long ago. Deep within she sensed a strange strength. What if she dared to hear and grasp the meaning of these words?

She lifted her head and met his gaze. Though he was far off she heard the message clearly, "Free yourself from the chains on your neck, O captive Daughter of Zion." He knew who she was. Now she knew Him as well: it was her Father calling to her. This messenger was sent by Him!

I believe this picture illustrates the condition of the majority of women in the body of Christ. Heirs — yet captive. Free — yet bound.

What did this poignant daughter see? How did she come to herself and realize her freedom?

I believe this book holds such a journey for you. I believe you have it in your hands for a reason and a purpose. This message will set free the daughters of Zion yet to be revealed, a generation awaiting their release. I see them lifting their heads, listening for the wind of the Holy Spirit.

I pray that through these truths you will find your freedom and realize your destiny. You may doubt me, but dare to believe your Father God.

The most desolate of wastelands
is our past. It holds no life, and
its arid soil is insatiable.

2

Rise Up
From the Dust

So much transpires in Isaiah 52:1-2 that I feel it is necessary to point out each step of God's process. Therefore we will examine it point by point, process by process. Let's go deeper and look closer at this woman and the message.

An Urgent Summons

"Awake, awake, O Zion..." It is important to note that the messenger repeats himself. This accomplished two purposes: 1) it awakened her from her slumber, and 2) it alerted her to her true condition.

The words snapped her from the sleep that shrouded her, pulling her from the dream in which she was hidden. She was trapped by her past yet afraid of her future. Stepping forward while always looking back.

Most mornings when I awaken my children for school, I

try to be pleasant, saying in a singsong voice, "Time to get up." I enjoy watching them stretch and turn their sleepy faces toward me as they blink at the morning light. I may even gently motivate them to move a little faster with, "Daddy's making pancakes." They smile and tumble from their bunks. The morning process has begun.

Then there are other mornings — the ones we've over-slept. My wake-up style is altogether different on those days. I storm into their rooms, flip on the light and command, "Wake up!" Once I know they can hear me, I inform them of the lateness of the hour and the urgency of the moment. "You're being picked up in fifteen minutes!" Their eyes pop open as they snap into action. There is no time for pan-cakes on these mornings. Everything is a push to get them out the door on time.

I remember being awakened in this manner when I was young. It was never pleasant. But it was far worse to wake up and realize you had already missed your ride. In one case you have a chance to beat the clock, but in the other the clock has already beaten you.

By sounding the wake-up call twice, I believe the mes-senger was saying, "Wake up! It is very late, and you are in danger of remaining captive!"

But this daughter of Zion was sleepy with oppression and depression. Withdrawn and alone. Restrained and weary. She wondered if she would ever be free.

Notice the messenger called her by name, O Zion. He wanted her to know for certain he was speaking directly to her. This was not a general alarm but a specific mandate. He knew who she was even though she thought she had been forgotten.

Get Dressed

He recognized her weakness and said, "Clothe yourself with strength." He did not offer to strengthen her but told her to strengthen herself. I'm sure she thought, *I have no strength*. When we come to the end of our own strength, we find God's strength. A captive prisoner has no natural strength to speak of. That was not the kind she needed. She needed inner strength, the type only God supplies. She needed to draw from His well of water, the source of strength deep inside, the spring that never fails. She lifted her head.

Pointing to the clothes that had been stripped from her the messenger urged, "Put on your garments of splendor." I believe these garments represent her crushed hopes and discarded dreams, those which constant disappointment and abuse snatched from her. This messenger thrust them back into her hands. She marveled that they had been kept safe and intact. She had feared she would never see them again. Clutching them in her hand she thought, *Do I dare? I failed when I was younger and stronger. I've been unfaithful. Are these still mine?*

The messenger sensed her fear and reassured her in more intimate terms, "O Jerusalem, the holy city. The uncircumcised and defiled will not enter you again."

With this he told her, "I know who you are, what you have done and what has happened to you." Then he addressed her fear of failure and recurring harassment. He assured her that no longer would she be raped, defiled and robbed of her dignity. She was holy, renewed and protected.

Zion represents all that is of Jewish descent. This includes the natural seed of Abraham, which is the nation of Israel, and the spiritual seed of Abraham, which is the church. The word *Jerusalem* in this passage points to the holy city "prepared as a bride adorned for her husband" (Rev. 21:2). The messenger spoke affectionately to restore her, calling her forth as a remnant of the whole.

Shake It Off

"Shake off your dust" signifies an aggressive removal of all that had dirtied or soiled her. The dust is the remains of past journeys and failures. Dust is carried in by the wind but accumulates in vacant stillness. It settles on barren ground void of vegetation and moisture, producing lands of famine. The most desolate of these wastelands is our past. It holds no life; its arid soil is insatiable, draining our very life.

This desperate woman sat surrounded by dust. Each new wind blew more her way — the dust of past wounds and failures. The longer we sit in our past and the more we study it, the more we are doomed to repeat it. We must shake it off.

The daughter of Zion brushed the dust from her shoulders and arms. She wiped it from her eyes and tossed it out of her hair.

Rise Up and Take Your Place

The messenger told her, "Rise up." She stood and left her past on the ground.

She was then told, "Sit enthroned, O Jerusalem."

The beloved of God is no longer to sit in her past mistakes, abuses and failures. A throne has been prepared for her. A position of delegated authority awaits her. She is to rest in this position, exercising and enjoying the rights and privileges it provides. This throne is for God's children, the broken and contrite.

Having delivered these pledges and promises the messenger exclaimed, "Free yourself from the chains on your neck, O captive daughter of Zion."

He acknowledged that she was indeed captive, but he let her know she did not have to remain that way. He assured her that it was within her power to free herself from the chains of bondage.

The chains did not bind her hands or feet nor did they encircle her waist. They encompassed and immobilized her neck. Even though she could fully move her arms and legs, she was tethered and restricted by the neck.

She moved cautiously, aware of her limits. Yet spurred on by the hope of freedom she began to feel for what she could not see. When she had shaken herself and brushed the dust from her garments, she thought she felt something.

So she lifted the collar of her tattered rags and reached toward her heart. Her chains had kept her from seeing it, but her finger could trace the outline of a key resting against her bosom. She pulled it out into the fading sunlight and turned it over in her hand. She had never seen the lock that sealed the yoke around her neck. All she could do was feel it. But she was certain this must be the key. Her Father had hidden it here for just such a time. She inserted the key into the lock, and with a rusty groan her chains fell at her feet.

So many of us are leashed to a wall. We move our arms and legs, but our activity takes us nowhere. We're held captive by the throat.

The key to freedom is already hidden in the hearts of those who dare to believe. It is not the key to something...but to Someone.

Behold I stand at the door and knock (Rev. 3:20).

It is up to us to use the key and unlock the door of our captive hearts.

You can spend your whole life figuring out why you are messed up and still be messed up once you've figured it out.

3

The Past Is
Not Your Future

Perhaps you felt you knew the woman in chapter 1. Possibly she reminded you of a friend, sister or relative. Maybe the connection ran even deeper: reflected in her you saw your own pain, frustration, broken dreams and captivity.

Like her you have been angered and frustrated by the messages of liberty that only caused you to feel more bound. Perhaps you groped for the hand of the messenger, hoping for assistance or support, only to find he had stepped beyond your reach. You have struggled but eventually settled back down into the dust of your past.

When you have come to an end of yourself you are ripe — no, desperate — for change. You may even now be saying, "I've tried so many times, and it has never worked!" I have a word from God for you: Your past is not your future.

If we measure our future by our past we are doomed to repeat it. It is a fallacy to believe that by studying our past failures, traumas or abuses we prevent or correct our current ones. Looking at our past does not guarantee our future — it prevents it. When we search, analyze and delve into our yesterdays, we are limited to our own accumulated information of abuse or wrong decisions. Drawing on our own wisdom and experience will not safeguard our future.

We need someone bigger and wiser than ourselves to guide and protect us — we need God. He knows the end from the beginning. He sees the whole picture clearly, while we see only a fragment dimly and distorted (1 Cor. 13:12). He is independent of time while we are subject to it. How can we draw on this wisdom?

First we must treat our past the way God prescribes. So how does God process our past? What is His instruction?

Your Past Is Gone

> Brothers, I do not consider myself yet to have taken hold of it. But one thing I do: Forgetting what is behind and straining toward what is ahead, I press on toward the goal to win the prize for which God has called me heavenward in Christ Jesus (Phil. 3:13-14).

One day the Holy Spirit spoke to me, contrasting this verse with what appears to be its present application. He warned, "The church is straining for what is behind and forgetting what is ahead."

When we stretch back and try to make sense of all that happened in the past, we are bound to be frustrated. Constantly replaying, reviewing and rewinding, we build different scenarios of what might have been. It's like trying to walk forward while looking backward. We think, *If only I had done this or that, things would have been different.* Yes, it is true, things would have been different. But you didn't do it differently, and thinking about it *now* can't change it *then.* Your past, no matter how tragic or terrible, is gone. You can never reach back into it and change it.

Even the wonderful parts of your past are gone. Don't try to live in them and allow them to drain your life in the present. It will only waste your time and energy.

God never goes back, though He is the only one who can. He goes forward. He is always looking ahead and moving beyond the present.

When Adam fell God did not sit down and think, *Where did I go wrong? I should never have planted that tree! I should have set up an angel to guard it. Now I'm going to have to start over. I'd better figure this out so it won't happen again.*

No, God explained to Adam and Eve the immediate and far-reaching consequences of their actions. Yet even in the midst of this sad separation He prophesied their redemption from the fall and the curse of sin (Gen. 3:15).

This is a tragic truth: You can spend your whole life figuring out why you are messed up and still be messed up once you've figured it out. After all your searching you know the *why.* But knowing the why does not produce the power to change. You must know the *Who.* You don't go to the problem for the answer. You must move from the problem to the answer. Our answer is Jesus. The question is, Do we believe what He did was enough?

Too often we allow the enemy to deceive us into believing our case is unique or our hurt is too big for God. We think, *I'm a special exception and therefore need to be handled differently.* So we gather all the information and tell our story, trying to discover why something happened. Unfortunately, knowing why doesn't necessarily mean we will ever make sense of what happened.

Forget It

Our friend, the woman in Isaiah 52:1-2, represents Israel when she was taken into captivity for forgetting God. The people had committed all types of idolatry, had broken every commandment He gave and were proud and haughty (see Is. 14:1).

In this captivity the Israelites felt hopeless and forlorn. They were afraid God would leave them in their bondage. Their guilt weighed so heavy on them that they doubted God could ever forgive their iniquity. As they looked around at the Babylonian citizens and the strange land of captivity, all they could do was remember what had been. Their failures were ever before them.

But when God spoke to them during this captivity He comforted them and painted a very different picture — one of hope. He wanted them to stir themselves to believe He would once again restore them. He told them to forget their past failures and unfaithfulness.

> Do not be afraid; you will not suffer shame. Do not fear disgrace; you will not be humiliated. You will forget the shame of your youth and remember no more the reproach of your widowhood (Is. 54:4).

God did not say, "I want you to remember your shame and learn from it." He said, "Forget about it because I have." He addressed their fears, admonishing them, "Don't be afraid. I won't let you be shamed, disgraced or humiliated. I won't remind you of your past so don't let anyone else — forget about it." In essence God was saying, "You once were that; now I have made you new; soon you'll be this!"

More Than We Expect

> See, I am doing a new thing! Now it springs up;
> do you not perceive it? I am making a way in the
> desert and streams in the wasteland (Is. 43:19).

God enjoys turning our wastelands into fertile plains. He has a plan for irrigating our arid land. He knows this plan; we do not.

Those who look back say, "Tomorrow will be like today because today was like yesterday." This is not how God views things. He understands that our human nature battles fear, so He encourages us.

> "For I know the plans I have for you," declares the
> Lord, "plans to prosper you and not to harm you,
> plans to give you hope and a future" (Jer. 29:11).

Notice that God does not outline the plan nor does He say, "You will know the plan." He only assures us He knows the plan, and it is good.

Of course we would like to hear the details. We want to know when, where, how and with whom. I have a theory that even if He told us all these specific details we still would ask why. So He gives no specifics and affords us the opportunity to trust Him.

We feel overwhelmed if we try to figure out all of these elements. We can't. We don't have the necessary information. Even when we think we've figured out the plan, God never does what we expect. In reality, He does more.

> Now to him who is able to do immeasurably more
> than all we ask or imagine, according to his power
> that is at work within us (Eph. 3:20).

Dare to believe when you cannot see or understand. Decide to trust God instead of dwelling on your fears. This is the powerful force that separates the believers from the unbelievers. Complete knowledge does not require faith. God challenges us simply to trust Him and His word.

My husband, John, always shares this truth, "Only one person can get you out of the will of God — you!" No man, woman, minister, ministry, parent, spouse or friend can do it. Only you. When you set yourself in agreement with God's will and plan for your life, the opinions of men, women, organizations and devils no longer matter. It does not matter how many times those around you have failed. It does not matter how many times you've failed. God never has.

If God is for you who can be against you? (Rom. 8:31). God's purpose will prevail — unless of course you choose not to believe.

If no one can get you out of God's will, then it is equally certain that only you can move into it. It is a decision you make on your own.

The Choice Is Yours

The most striking point of Isaiah 52 is that the woman's freedom utterly depended upon *her* taking action, not God. It was her response to God's directive that determined her destiny. God had already supplied everything she needed to attain her freedom, but she had to act on the message. It had to be mixed with faith. It was now her choice — to believe or remain bound.

Often we make others responsible. We want them to help us. We look to family, friends or ministries, thinking if we just could get close enough to them we would be free. But usually the closer we get, the more flaws we see. We then realize they too are only human and must depend upon God. They tumble off pedestals upon which they never should have been placed. Their demise often leaves us feeling disillusioned.

God allows this for a reason. He wants us to look at the message, not the messenger. He wants to receive all the glory for what He does in our lives. We are granted the privilege of laboring with Him in this process. He trains our hands for war and our fingers for battle (Ps. 144:1).

When we set our hearts to pursue God and all that He has provided, all hell trembles. It is then that the enemy releases his onslaught of discouragement. Constantly trying to turn us back, he points to our past failures and fears. Discouraged, we often mistake the enemy's resistance as God's refusal to help us.

God is not refusing; He is waiting on us. Decide today that you will no longer tolerate captivity. Do not live in less than what Jesus' death provided. You are to reign with Him. Choose His life.

I felt impressed to close this chapter with this word of encouragement from my journal. These words were specific to me, but I also give Scripture references so you can see how they apply to you. God never contradicts His Word. This is something the Lord gave to me in prayer. Let it minister hope to you.

Journal Excerpt

> *I know you feel empty and dry, My child, and this emptying is of Me. I am removing the last of the old, but do not move to the soul. Stay in the spirit. Spring up, O well! Call that well forth. Ask Me for rain. Call out for My refreshing. You are on the threshold and in need of My strength to put you over. Worship and praise before Me. Let your mind be still. This will be your strength and refreshing.*
>
> *Do not plan out or premeditate but know that I*

will cause those who have risen up against you to be ashamed and confounded before you. Only do not be afraid nor allow terror to creep in as before, but gird yourself with love and praise. Guard what you hear and say for the enemy longs to sow tares of strife. Be of few words for you will have little to say until I fill your mouth, but soon you will break forth in an overflow.

Before you go any further, boldly pray this with me:

This day I make a decision to fear and honor You, God, above all my past failures and over all that would seek to discourage or distract me.

Scriptures related to the journal excerpt: Num. 21:17; Ps. 35:4; 138:2; 141:3; Is. 52:9; Jer. 1:17-19; Matt. 13:36-43; John 4:13-14; 1 John 4:18.

Some of us have put up with
captivity and harassment so long
it has become a way of life.

4

It Is Time to
Get Restless

N ow that we've established how the daughter of Zion
is set free, the question is, When will she loose herself of her chains?

> But when you grow restless, you will throw his
> yoke from off your neck (Gen. 27:40).

Notice it did not say, "When God thinks you can't take it
anymore He will take the yoke off you." Nor did it say,
"When God decides you have suffered enough He will
remove the yoke." In fact, God is not even mentioned in
this verse, but we find the words *you* or *your* are mentioned
three times.

Paraphrased, it could read, "When you've had enough
you will throw off your bondage. When you've stopped
blaming everyone else; when you stop feeling sorry for
yourself; when you stop searching for a person or organiza-

tion to help you; when you no longer look back; when you stop blaming God; when you are finally frustrated with the limitations of your yoke; when you are tired enough to get mad; then you'll break free."

This verse of scripture comes from the story of Jacob and Esau, the twin sons of Isaac. Esau was the oldest and had the right to receive a special blessing from his father. Yet Jacob usurped his brother's blessing. Unknowingly, Isaac gave Jacob all that was good and set him up as master over Esau.

When Esau learned of this, he wept and pleaded with Isaac for some word of blessing. The only blessing Isaac could bestow on Esau was, "But when you grow restless, you will throw his yoke from off your neck" (Gen 27:40).

It is important to note that God did not take away Esau's blessing without reason. Esau forfeited it to Jacob years earlier when he had come back from a hunting trip faint with hunger. He asked Jacob for some of his stew. Seeing that Esau was vulnerable, Jacob asked for the birthright in exchange. "Look, I am about to die," Esau said. "What good is the birthright to me?" He swore an oath to him, selling his birthright to Jacob. So Esau despised his birthright (Gen. 25: 29-34).

Another translation says Esau treated his birthright as common. He did not respect or honor the covenant relationship he had inherited as a descendant of Abraham. He esteemed it lightly and toyed with it. He sold out his spiritual heritage for temporary, natural comfort.

Esau represents natural favor, strength, talent and ability. He was the firstborn. He even had a natural covering of hair. He represents all that a man can achieve in his natural ability. He had the arm of the flesh (2 Chr. 32:8). He appealed to his fathers taste for the wild.

Isaac, who had a taste for wild game, loved Esau, but Rebekah loved Jacob (Gen. 25: 28).

Jacob, on the other hand, did not have the physical skill that would endear him to Isaac, but he was loved by Rebekah. He was a quiet man who hung out in the tents. He was closer to his mother, possibly because he knew his father preferred Esau. I'm sure she encouraged him and told him what God had shown her when she was pregnant: the older would serve the younger (Gen. 25:23). Jacob represents the weaker and less obvious. God does not promote or reward in the manner of man. Even though Jacob was weaker in strength and ability, hidden within him was the strength to become a prince of God. Jacob overcame his weakness and was given a new name, *Israel,* which means "prince of God" (Gen. 32:28).

Some of us have been mastered by circumstances and by those around us. This has happened because we have not taken seriously our covenant and the authority it bears. When we are careless with a covenant we run the risk of losing its protection and benefits.

This is true of any covenant relationship — marriage, family or leadership. When we do not use our authority, someone else will take it from us and use it against us. All authority comes from God and is delegated (Luke 9:1). Therefore, to have authority you must be under authority.

Esau came out from under his father's authority, protection and blessing; Jacob's blessing became a curse to Esau. He was now subjected to his brother.

The authority of God is present in our lives whether we use it or not. God has given us the authority of the name of Jesus. It is both a privilege and an honor to share His name and the dominion it represents. But if we do not take our place or if we sell out to the temporary at the expense of the eternal, we leave the door open for another to usurp our authority. Our God-given authority is then used against us, not for us.

The Bible said Jesus took all of Satan's authority. He

stripped him of his keys and armor (Luke 11:22; Rev. 1:18). Therefore the only authority Satan has is what he tricks us into yielding. The only weapons he wields are the ones we lay aside.

He comes at us with, "You can't use that weapon. You're not clean enough, or holy enough," and reminds us of our past failures. He intimidates us into measuring our worth by our past performance. If we assess ourselves by these standards, we discover we are weak and lacking in righteousness. So we listen and believe Satan's lies. Then we lay down our weapons.

But our covenant is not based on our ability or righteousness. It is based on Jesus' triumph and His righteousness. Our covenant with God is one of grace built on better promises (Heb. 8:6). It is important that we honor and esteem it as such. Always dare to believe. We must fear and honor God enough never to sell out for temporary comfort or relief.

Go Ahead, Get Mad

After John and I were married for one year, he quit a secure engineering position with good pay to take a service position at our local church. His earnings were almost half of what they had been previously. At that point I waved goodbye to the idea of ever owning a house.

As a couple we had agreed to lay aside our financial security and pursue in earnest the call of God on our lives. No sooner than we set our hearts to do so, our finances came under attack from every direction. One morning I went out to my car and found the window shattered in pieces on the car seat. There was no apparent reason for the break, so we had to blame it on the relentless Texas heat. The car was not fit to drive, and we did not have the money to fix it.

I took a job to help out, but the onslaught seemed to

drain everything. No longer was I dreaming wistfully of a house. I was worried if I would have enough to buy gas and food until the next paycheck came.

John and I tithed faithfully and gave offerings, yet it seemed we were robbed on every side. One night we attended a service where people were testifying about God's faithfulness in blessing their finances. I thought to myself, *I don't care about blessing. At this point I would just like provision.* After the service we both were so discouraged that we sat in John's car and cried. We promised each other not even to hint about our financial need to anyone. If God did not take care of us, we would do without.

The next day while home for lunch, I read all the scriptures I could find about finances and provision. Frustrated, I stomped my foot and said aloud, "God, You said You'd meet my needs. Well, You're not!"

He answered back, "I am not standing between you and your finances."

I was bewildered. I knew we were doing everything on our end to keep the covenant we had made with God. We had confessed, believed, given offerings and tithed. The only thing we had not done was receive. God had told me He was not withholding the finances from us. So who was?

Then I got mad. Right there in my kitchen I yelled, "It is written that God will meet my needs according to His riches in glory. These are needs. Devil, I command you to get your hands off our finances. We will not back down from the call of God upon our lives. Let God be true no matter what it looks like."

I actually felt something happen within me. I was excited and hopeful even though I had not done anything except stand in my kitchen and shout. I called John at the office and said, "Honey, something has happened. God is not the problem. The devil is!" John was so excited. God had shown him the same thing on his lunch hour. We both rejoiced. We were rich in faith.

That night after service, a couple who had visited the church pulled us aside. They shared that God had told them to give us some money. Then they handed us an envelope and left. When we got home we were shocked to discover it contained what we needed to fix my car with enough left over to buy groceries and gas.

Some of you need to yell in your kitchen! You have put up with harassment and captivity so long it has become a way of life. Don't let timidity and past failures hold you down. God is not holding out on you! He is cheering you on!

When my boys first started to walk, they enjoyed venturing the short distance from sofa to table. They would walk farther if we all cheered and clapped. They would stand and screech to get everyone's attention, take a few steps and clap for themselves.

But the day came when they realized walking was not just for show, it was for keeps. Suddenly they did not think it was so much fun. They had to work hard to keep up the pace. They would plop down on their diapered bottoms and wail for someone to pick them up so they could ride on a hip.

Often I would move out of reach and encourage them, "Come on, you can do it!" They knew they could, but it was easier not to. They wanted to be carried.

Now I can't slow them down. Walking is no longer a problem. They are running everywhere! They even do things on Rollerblades that scare me! They discovered the joy of independent mobility. When they got tired of sitting and waiting to be picked up, they stood, walked and then ran.

Don't sit on the floor waiting for someone to pick you up. If you are restless, God is calling you not only to walk but to run — free and untethered. You don't have to wait for the next seminar to cut loose. You don't have to figure it all out first. Just get mad and get free!

Allow the faith of God to open your eyes to see what doubt and discouragement have hidden from your view.

Journal Excerpt

My child, you must not hide yourself and draw back. With everything that is in you, you must press closer. Do not despair or hold yourself according to past failures for there is a new grace on you to rise up and defeat the hindrances in your life. Move swiftly and surely as this time of preparation is at hand. You must learn now for it will not be as easy later. Keep joy as your strength and subject your flesh until it is your servant. A new liberty and strength will come upon you as this is accomplished. Do not be discouraged but encouraged in Me.

Scriptures related to the journal excerpt: 1 Sam. 30:6; Neh. 8:10; Ps. 42:5; 73:28; Rom. 5:16-17; 6:19; Phil. 3:13; James 4:8.

God is wooing a bride
from among His church,
one who loves Him because
she cannot live without Him.

5

Is Jesus Coming for a Wife or a Bride?

When a man marries a bride she becomes his wife, right? Yes, this is true. But is it possible to be a wife and not be a bride? Most of us know the definition of a wife, but what about a bride? We were brides for such a short time we have forgotten what it was like altogether.

Companionship

When John and I were engaged, I was his bride. We were head over heels in love with each other for no reason other than we felt made for each other. We were certain God had brought us together. We counted the days and hours that separated us and anxiously anticipated our time together. When we were with each other nothing else seemed to matter. All other pressures or distractions seemed to fall away.

John did not ask me to marry him because I was a good

cook, a great mother, a good housekeeper, financially responsible or a wonderful helpmate. I had not proved I could be any of these things. He had not required I prove my aptitude in any area. He knew he had my heart and that was enough for him.

He proposed because he loved me and felt incomplete without me. It did not seem to matter whether I would ever bear a child, keep a house, balance a checkbook or stand beside him in ministry. He married me for one reason — companionship.

God brought Eve out of Adam's side for this same reason. Adam was lonely for someone who was like himself. God put Adam into a deep sleep and removed a rib from his side, which God used to create Eve. Then God presented her to Adam (Gen. 2:21-23). Eve had been hidden in Adam all along. They came together again as one but in a new and different way — separate and yet one.

In the same way, the Father has prepared us as the bride of Christ. The death of Christ, the second Adam, brought forth His bride, the church. Christ's side was pierced, and the blood and water flowed as He entered into the sleep of death. Now we, as the bride, anxiously await the marriage supper of the Lamb where we will see Him face-to-face and be joined together with Him forever.

God's grace is truly amazing, for His mercy triumphs over our judgment. Though we deserved death, He redeemed us to be His only Son's bride and companion forever. This positions us as His children.

He did not redeem us to enslave us. It is for freedom that Christ has set us free (Gal. 5:3). He does not want us to work *for* Him. He redeemed us so that we may work *alongside* Him. We can do nothing of eternal value apart from Him, so it is foolish to think we can do anything *for* Him. We only produce what is acceptable and life-giving when we work *with* Him, through His strength, His life and His Spirit.

Acceptable Offering

Abel's sacrifice was accepted because he followed the pattern God had established in the garden. An innocent animal was to be slain and offered to cover the nakedness and transgressions of man.

Abel was a keeper of sheep. God supplied the grass, grain and water that nourished Abel's flocks. Abel only tended them. At the appointed time Abel separated the first-born lamb from his flock to give to the Lord.

His brother Cain labored as a tiller of the ground. He planted, cultivated, tended and harvested his crops, but when God rejected the offering from his crops, he was enraged and became jealous of his brother.

> Then the Lord said to Cain, "Why are you angry? Why is your face downcast? If you do what is right, will you not be accepted? But if you do not do what is right, sin is crouching at your door; it desires to have you, but you must master it" (Gen. 4:6-7).

God did not reject Cain — He rejected his offering. Cain was not able to make that distinction. He felt rejected and isolated. God noticed this and encouraged him to do right and overcome this sin which crouched at his door. Cain had the same opportunity as Abel to present an acceptable sacrifice, but Cain did not listen to God's advice.

More than likely Adam had instructed his sons that animal sacrifice was the acceptable method of preparing an offering for God. Otherwise, how would Abel have known what to do? Perhaps animal sacrifice seemed too simple to Cain. Maybe he wanted to present something he had produced to God. Whatever the reason, it appeared Cain was too busy laboring for God to labor with Him.

It is easier to attack those around us than to admit we

have done things in our own way and by our own strength. So Cain rose up and killed the brother he believed God favored.

> Now Cain said to his brother Abel, "Let's go out to the field." And while they were in the field, Cain attacked his brother Abel and killed him (Gen. 4:8).

His Labor or Ours?

When we work *for* God instead of *with* God, we lose sight of God's character, nature and perspective. Our motives become distorted and mixed. We become proud of our accomplishments (look how hard I have worked), religious (serve God our way instead of His), legalistic (by the parameters and restrictions of man) and judgmental (critical of all outside our understanding). Soon we are presenting the works of our hands and the labor of our flesh to God for His blessing. But He will not bless that.

Frustrated, we begin to strive with our brothers. Envy stirs our hearts against those who are laboring acceptably. We are tempted to believe we deserve more because we are working harder. Why should they be blessed? The enemy wants to deceive us into believing they have removed or displaced the favor we feel is due us.

God's favor and acceptance are available to everyone, but they are given on His terms, not ours. God imparts a righteousness born of the Spirit and contrary to our natural reason (Gal. 5:5). It cannot be earned by works; therefore it cannot be kept by them. It is a gift. We receive it based on Jesus' righteousness and God's love.

Religion is restrictive and self-righteous. It labors to produce while the Spirit produces without labor. Unfortunately, many in the church are busy being "religious wives" while God is waiting and watching for a loving bride.

I believe God is wooing a bride from among His church — one who loves Him because she cannot live without Him.

Bride Versus Wife

To explain the concept of being a bride, let's look at the story of Hannah. Hannah was one of the two wives of Elkanah. She is mentioned first, which indicates he married her first. It was probably due to Hannah's barrenness that Elkanah chose to marry a second wife, Peninnah. Elkanah's second wife bore him many children, while Hannah's barrenness continued for years. Hannah was loved and cared for by her husband, yet there was a hunger stirring in her for more. This was evident when the family went to worship before the Lord.

> Whenever the day came for Elkanah to sacrifice, he would give portions of the meat to his wife Peninnah and to all her sons and daughters. But to Hannah he gave a double portion because he loved her, and the Lord had closed her womb. And because the Lord had closed her womb, her rival kept provoking her in order to irritate her. This went on year after year. Whenever Hannah went up to the house of the Lord, her rival provoked her till she wept and would not eat (1 Sam. 1:4-7).

Even though Hannah was honored by her husband with a double portion, she could not enjoy it because she was so tormented by her adversary. How could God allow this? Notice it was God, not the devil, who closed Hannah's womb. Why? I believe God closed it to create a divine hunger in Hannah, one greater than a child could satisfy, one only He could fulfill.

Hannah loved her husband, but she had learned through

the adversity she experienced that he was not her source of life. God was. She watched as Peninnah bore her husband's sons. Elkanah's name was established, yet still she hungered for more. No matter how wonderful her husband was to her, it was not enough to fill the gnawing void in her heart.

Brokenness and humility were woven into Hannah's nature. All the longing, disappointment and torment created a womb that could bear a prophetic seed.

I believe Hannah was a bride. Because God was her source of life, she was a giver, not a taker. This is why her husband loved Hannah more than Peninnah, even though it appeared she produced less.

Year after year she prayed for a son. At first her motive might have been, "God give me a son for my husband's name sake." Then it may have changed to, "God, give me a son because of my adversary." But when it became, "God, give me son, and I will give him to You," God gave her her desire.

Hannah made a vow, saying:

> O Lord Almighty, if you will only look upon your servant's misery and remember me, and not forget your servant but give her a son, then I will give him to the Lord for all the days of his life, and no razor will ever be used on his head (1 Sam. 1:11).

Hannah had called the life of God into an empty barren womb. Not just the natural life of a child, but of one set apart and inspired by God. Out of her despair she consecrated and conceived the child Samuel. He was the prophetic voice of God to a lost and straying Israel.

Both women were married to the same husband but with very different relationships. Peninnah was the religious wife while Hannah was the lovestruck bride. Following are some contrasts between these two women:

Hannah	Peninnah
Barren	Fruitful
Loved	Used
Broken	Proud
Godly	Religious
Self-denying	Self-seeking
Bride	Wife

Hannah was barren and loved while Peninnah was fruitful and used. Hannah was broken, and sought God, not just religious activities. Peninnah was proud of her offspring and comfortable with the religious. She despised Hannah because Hannah was loved by Elkanah even though she produced no children. Hannah denied herself the joy of raising her child in order to give him to the Lord. Peninnah appeared to be concerned only with herself and cared nothing for the feelings of others. Hannah was her husband's love while Peninnah was his wife.

After Samuel, Hannah bore five more children while Peninnah had no more (1 Sam. 2:21). She had already fulfilled her purpose.

It would appear Hannah's nature and motives were very different from Peninnah's. We glimpse Peninnah's nature in her prophetic prayer on the advent of Samuel's dedication:

> Do not keep talking so proudly or let your mouth speak such arrogance, for the Lord is a God who knows, and by him deeds are weighed. Those who were full hire themselves out for food, but those who were hungry hunger no more. She who was barren has borne seven children, but she who has had many sons pines away (1 Sam. 2:3,5).

Peninnah had comforted herself with the children she had produced. She had been full while Hannah had hungered.

Now Peninnah watched as her children were displaced by the children of Hannah, the favored wife.

I believe these two wives prophetically represent the condition of the church. There are barren brides crying out for more, and there are satisfied wives who remain silent. The brides love and are loved by God. They are intimate with Him. They have been broken and humbled by their adversaries. The persecution wrought the godly character of meekness into their nature. They will not touch the glory, but return it all back to God. They have not forgotten why they love — they are His bride.

How's Your Appetite?

What I have seen God do in the past and what I see Him doing right now is wonderful. But I am hungry for something I have yet to see, taste or handle. I rejoice for what the body of Christ has experienced, but I hunger for more.

This desire for more began to stir in my heart until I felt I was pregnant with it. Then God challenged me: "If you want more than what you've seen, you'll need to be more than you've been. You'll need to give more than you've given." At each new level in our walks with God there is an increase of commitment and separation.

One morning as I prayed for my family, I asked God to increase my children's hunger for Him. Deep in my spirit I heard His response, "If your children are not hungry, it is because they are already full."

Just as natural hunger comes when we are empty and leaves when we are full, so it is with the hunger of the Spirit. Therefore, I will only be hungry when I am not already full. To develop this spiritual hunger I will need to fast all that is not of God that tries to fill me. To explain, let's look again at Hannah.

Hannah fasted her double portion of food and favor, and prostrated herself before God. She refused to be comforted merely by the favor of man. She wanted the favor of God. In her day barrenness was a reproach. When her husband gave her a double portion of meat at the religious feast, it said to those present, "I love this woman. Though she has not borne me a child, she has my favor." But Hannah had come to the place where this double portion of her husband's love and favor was not enough. So she cried out to God, aware that only His provision could satisfy her.

In the midst of religious activities and worldly distractions it is important that we deny ourselves their fleeting satisfactions and cry out for more. Like Hannah, we need to cry out to the Most High until He answers our deepest yearnings. We are to deny our souls the satisfaction of the temporal and cry out for the eternal.

> A satisfied soul loathes the honeycomb, but to a hungry soul every bitter thing is sweet (Prov. 27:7, NKJV).

This example is not merely limited to food. To those who hunger for God, even His correction is refreshing. That is why the barren woman can sing.

> "Sing, O barren woman, you who never bore a child; burst into song, shout for joy, you who were never in labor; because more are the children of the desolate woman than of her who has a husband," says the Lord (Is. 54:1).

God is calling us back to our first love. There we will find the strength and sustenance to remain a bride.

John and I have four children. All were born out of intimacy. We were not intimate in order to have children. We have children because we have been intimate. Likewise, God wants our spiritual offspring to be the product of intimacy with Him. We are not to pursue Jesus in order to get salvation, finances, ministry, anointing, healing or anything else. All these are found when we lose ourselves in Him.

About five years ago while I prepared to minister at a women's meeting, I prayed my same old, pious prayer: "God, just use me to minister to these women..." God interrupted me with a question.

"Lisa, have you ever been used by a friend?"

"Yes," I answered hesitantly.

"How did you like it?"

"I didn't. I felt betrayed."

"Have you ever been used by a boyfriend?"

"Yes," I answered.

"How did you like it?"

"I didn't. I felt cheap and dirty."

Then God replied, "I don't use people. Satan does. I heal them, anoint them, transform and conform them to My image, but I do not use them."

I was shocked. I had always been taught to pray that way, but suddenly I could see how absurd it was to think of God as a user and a taker.

God told me that it grieves Him when ministers allow Him only limited access into a few areas of their ministry while barring His access to other areas. The area most frequently denied is His influence in our personal lifestyles.

The areas we hold back from God eventually become our downfall. I don't know how many times I have heard someone say, "I just don't understand how someone who was so anointed to preach could become an alcoholic or abuse his or her family or commit adultery. God had used him or her so mightily. How could this happen?"

It is always God's desire to flow through every area of our being, not just in the area of ministry. We are the ones who limit God. It is my prayer that His anointing will spill into every area of my life, that not one area will remain untouched by His presence.

Known by God

> We know that we all possess knowledge. Knowledge puffs up, but love builds up. The man who thinks he knows something does not yet know as he ought to know. But the man who loves God is known by God (1 Cor. 8:1-3).

It is not the amount of knowledge we have that produces life. Life is found in the knowledge that we live. Is it better to have knowledge of God or to be known by Him? You can know about someone but still not have a relationship with that person. It is of utmost importance that we are known by God.

When Jesus spoke in the Gospels about entrance to the kingdom of heaven being denied to someone, it was followed by this explanation: "Depart, I do not know you." They knew Him, but He did not know them. How tragic to know about someone without ever taking the time to let that person know you.

The psalmist cried, "Search me, O God, and know my heart" (Ps. 139:23). He wanted God to delve into the deepest recesses of his soul until he was known by God. It is in this process that we are transformed by the light of His Word. It is through this process that we develop a heart that can love God. We are transformed from wives to brides. May you hunger to know even as you are known so that you might love even as you are loved.

Journal Excerpt

> *I love you. I want you to rejoice in this. Freely receive this love and correction at My hand and by My side. Do not run from Me but to Me, for you are grafted and must not tear or strain our bond but*

simply walk alongside Me. Run when I run; rest as I rest; climb as I climb; leap as I leap. Up, over and onward toward your destiny to become like Me. This destiny will be forged and strengthened at My side. Do not try this in your own strength. You'll only come back to Me disappointed when it fails you. For the work that I do is swift and sure, and yields much joy and fruit. Partake of both as you go, for I would not have you weary and void of strength but refreshed with and by our labor. My ways are not burdensome but easy and light, perfected by obedience and love. So sit at My feet and learn of Me.

Scriptures related to the journal excerpt: Matt. 11:29-30; Luke 10:41-42; Rom. 8:29; 11:17-21; Phil. 2:12-13; Hab. 12:5-6.

If you are receiving your affirmation,
love, self-worth, joy, strength and
acceptance from anywhere but God,
He will shake it.

6

Shake Us
to Wake Us

When God shakes us to wake us, we often find ourselves surrounded by the unfamiliar and unfriendly.
God wakes us up from the secure by pushing us out
of our comfort zone. By comfort zone I am referring to all
that is familiar, expected, constant and under our own control.

We are comfortable when what we expect happens. We
enjoy being understood and supported by those around us.
We prefer to have a constant source of financial provision.
But when we get all this comfort and support, we are easily
lulled into a false sense of security.

God is more concerned with our condition than our comfort. At times He stirs our nests to make our comforting
things uncomfortable.

[The Lord is] like an eagle that stirs up its nest and

hovers over its young, that spreads its wings to catch them and carries them on its pinions (Deut. 32:11).

This is how young eagles get their flight training. They are born into a very comfortable and safe nest, padded and insulated with down from their mother. Meals are flown in fresh daily. But the day comes when their very survival is threatened if they stay in this place of comfort. So the mother eagle makes the welcoming and safe nest uncomfortable and unwelcome.

The mother eagle grabs the nest with her talons and flaps her wings up and down, blowing all the nice, comfortable padding out of the nest. She tears up what she had so carefully provided. Then she takes each baby eagle and carries it outside of the nest into the wind. This is where young eagles learn to fly. You can't try your wings if you're sitting in the nest.

When God's flight training began in earnest in my life, I felt as if there was nothing to hold on to. It seemed my life was a sea of uncertainty. Everything that had been constant was in upheaval or transition. At times it was so intense I would lay in bed, straining my brain trying to figure out why all this upheaval was happening.

Our finances were lacking. Socially we were shunned. I felt alone, isolated, misunderstood and persecuted. I prayed and cried out to the Lord for direction, only to hear my unanswered questions echoing back at me. I could find no rest.

I felt so conspicuous, as if I were walking around with a huge sign over my head that everyone but me could read. My neediness was so apparent that it repelled people. No one around us seemed to understand why or what we were going through.

I had long since grown weary of trying to explain myself

in order to get counsel or some word from the Lord. It seemed no one could help me. There was a reason for that. No one was supposed to. God wanted me to find my answers in Him. He was creating a hunger and restlessness in me.

John was going through the fire too. At first we would try to discuss it. Maybe we should do this. Perhaps we should never have left Dallas. We are under attack! Soon we found it too confusing to discuss.

John recognized that we were going through a refining process. But I questioned every aspect and detail, trying to make sense of it.

No Shortcut

One morning John came in excitedly from his time of prayer. God had spoken to him. *At least one person in our house could still hear from God,* I thought excitedly, so I was all ears.

John told me he had been out in a vacant field praying when God instructed him to look around. John noticed a section of short weed grass, then a large plot of dirt followed by an expanse of tall grass.

God told John the short grass represented the anointing he had known on his life; the dirt represented a wilderness he would go through; and the tall grass represented the anointing John would walk in after the wilderness.

I got excited, thinking we were almost through the lonely wilderness time of upheaval. John asked God where he was in the process, wondering if he was near the end of the dirt.

But God was very clear in His answer. "You are at the end of the short grass."

Disappointed, I questioned John, "Is that edifying? Am I supposed to be happy to hear that things are only going to get worse before they get better?" I wanted a shortcut through the dirt.

Soon I became so busy looking for a way out that I

missed the purpose of the process. I was so focused on the desert that I didn't see that the desert was forging the answer to my prayers — that God would create a clean heart in me and that He would separate the precious from the vile.

One particular evening while feeling exceptionally sorry for myself, I climbed into my bathtub and began to cry. I was six months pregnant with our second son. It appeared quite possible that John could lose his job. I felt persecuted and misunderstood. We believed we were obeying God, so why was all this happening?

John happened to come in and find his large, pregnant wife crying in the tub. He did not even need to ask me what I was crying about. When he looked at me I just poured out every fear, doubt, worry and question I had. "Why, why, why?" I asked.

Calmly John asked me, "Lisa, what have you asked God to do in your life? Did you ask for furniture or clothes?"

At that moment I was silently wishing I had asked for blessings instead of what I was going through.

John probed further, "What did you ask for?"

"I asked God to refine me," I mumbled back.

"Well, that is what you are getting," John answered and walked out.

I knew John was right. It just wasn't what I wanted to hear at the time. I wanted John to say something like, "You poor baby. Here you are pregnant and afraid I'm going to lose my job. Let me comfort you." I did not want him talking to me like I was a congregation. I wanted sympathy.

"God, even my husband doesn't understand me. Why are You putting me through a transition while I am pregnant?" I complained.

He answered, "Because it is the time when you feel the most vulnerable."

He was definitely right. I felt extremely vulnerable. I was

shaky, and He was doing the shaking. God will take the seasons when we feel weak and insecure and use them for our benefit.

> At that time his voice shook the earth, but now he has promised, "Once more I will shake not only the earth but also the heavens." The words "once more" indicate the removing of what can be shaken — that is, created things — so that what cannot be shaken may remain (Heb. 12:26-27).

I was uncomfortable because I was experiencing God's shaking in every aspect of my life. His shaking removes what is temporary and leaves only what is of His kingdom (v. 28). I have since learned to appreciate this process. I want to share five things that shaking accomplishes.

1.   It wakes you.

When my children are in a deep sleep, I often have to shake them to rouse them from their slumber. God does the same with His children — waking by shaking. Shaking is definitely not the most pleasant manner in which to be awakened, but it has the most effect. We become wide awake with our attention captured.

2.   It harvests what is ripe.

I live in Florida where there are plenty of orange groves. When it is citrus harvest time, the citrus growers use machinery with a mechanical arm to grab hold of the trunk of a tree and shake it. The ripe fruit falls into the waiting nets below. Only what is ripe falls freely. God's shaking harvests what is ripe in the life of a believer, both good and bad. We see the product of seeds previously planted.

3. It removes what is dead.

When the wind blows hard enough, it shakes dead leaves from the trees. Dead limbs and branches are also scattered in the wind. Only what is alive stays on the tree and survives the storm.

When God shakes us, only the things of His kingdom will remain. God shakes us to remove our dead works and lifeless limbs. There is no reason to fear the removal of what is old or dead. This paves the way for the new and living. God knows dead works weigh us down and become a fire hazard.

> His work will be shown for what it is, because the Day will bring it to light. It will be revealed with fire, and the fire will test the quality of each man's work (1 Cor. 3:13).

4. It strengthens and establishes.

What endures the shaking and remains afterward will be closer to its foundation.

My husband and I once took an international flight that had a layover on the island of Guam, which had just undergone a severe earthquake. All over the island, hotels were in ruins because the builders had not gone to the expense of digging deep enough to find a solid foundation of stone. The buildings shifted during the earthquake and sank until they hit something solid.

Our foundation is to be Jesus Christ. All we labor to build that is not supported by Him will suffer loss.

> For no one can lay any foundation other than the one already laid, which is Jesus Christ...If what he has built survives, he will receive his reward (1 Cor. 3:11,14).

God shakes so that the things which cannot be shaken will remain. His shaking removes all that is superfluous and that separates or entangles us. This allows us the opportunity to build anew on the proper support structure — Christ.

5. It unifies.

Imagine putting a cup of red sand and a cup of blue sand into a jar and shaking it. You get purple sand. It would be nearly impossible to separate the red sand from the blue sand again.

When God shakes the church it unites us. We wake up, stop the petty fights and realize what is important.

When we go through a personal shaking, we are knit closer to God. The bonds forged through suffering are harder to break than those made in good times. In the good times we often miss God's presence because we are surrounded by so many others who profess their support and undying loyalty. But when we're suffering, only He remains faithful, strengthening the bond of His love.

God Rebuilds

A note of warning: When God has shaken an area in your life, don't try to rebuild it yourself. Allow Him to restore only those things He wants to establish in your life. Remember, He is the one doing the shaking.

He is shaking our homes to find out what they are grounded on. This shaking will expose any hidden idols in our lives. An idol is what we give our strength to or draw our strength from.

If you are receiving your affirmation, love, self-worth, joy, strength and acceptance from anywhere but God, He will shake it. He does not do this to upset you; He does it so you will get your life from Him. He knows everything else

find your self worth from God not people or accomplishment

will eventually disappoint you.

After a shaking we see our condition in relation to God's truth. We see ourselves in comparison to God's standard. When we submit to God's truth we experience freedom. Liberty remains if we become responsible and accountable. It is not the truth you know but the truth you live that sets you free. To be responsible we must be obedient.

We would not grant as much liberty to a disobedient or rebellious child as we would grant to an obedient and responsible child. A disobedient child would use his liberty to rebel. He would confuse rebellion for freedom. Rebellion does not foster liberty; it brings bondage. Only through obedience can we find true liberty. As the Holy Spirit ministers truth to your heart, receive it and walk in it. Let God's Word be made flesh in your life.

Journal Excerpt

> *I have placed My hand upon you. The same hand that brings anointing also applies pressure. So do not resist My work in you. It is a good work to refine and strengthen, change and renew. A new thing I will do in you, a new flame I will kindle. I am preparing a vessel for this flame. A lamp for that light, one that is not tinted and does not obstruct the light. I will give you rest, My child, so fear not; lean upon Me as we travel swiftly to this new place.*

Scriptures related to the journal excerpt: Is. 41:13; 43:19; Matt. 5:14-16; 11:28; 25:1-13; 2 Tim. 2:21.

PART II

The Fruit of Fear

The real you is not the image
reflected in your mirror.

7

You Are Not
What You See!

When you look in your mirror, what do you see? Chances are, like most women, you can compile an immediate list of shortcomings, flaws, and wrinkles punctuated by a couple of assets. Your natural assessment may be correct, but you need to know something: What you see is not who you are.

You are someone no one sees — not your husband, your friends or even your parents. The real you is invisible to the scrutiny of the natural eye and often misrepresented by your outward actions. The real you is not the image greeting you in the mirror. Our outward image can never accurately reflect our inward nature. Our true life is hidden.

One day while critically assessing my reflection I heard the Holy Spirit ask, "What do you see?"

I promptly answered, "A tired, stressed mother."

He gently reminded me, "You are not what you see."

I immediately argued, looking closer in the mirror, "I am tired, and I am stressed, and I do look it!"

Again I heard, "You are not what you see."

True, I felt tired and stressed, but that was not who I was — it was what I felt. My reflection was true, but it was not the truth. My feelings and conditions are subject to change while God's truth remains unchanged and anchored in His Word. I am spirit, not body. I have a body, but I am not a body. I was assessing myself by what I had, not by who I was.

A Revealing Position

Earlier in my life I enjoyed a unique career as a promotional representative for a top cosmetic line. I was also a television makeup artist on the weekends. Representing the cosmetic line, I traveled an eight-state territory. Nearly every Monday morning I boarded a plane to visit a new city. I would do makeovers on women all week and return to Dallas on Friday afternoon. It was wonderful. I stayed in the finest hotels, enjoyed room service, a bubble bath and about three hours of Bible reading nightly. Best of all, my days were spent making woman feel better about themselves.

I had always enjoyed playing with makeup, but beyond that, I had developed it as a talent in order to hide my own flaws. I lost my right eye to cancer at the age of five, and the size and shape of my artificial eye differed from that of my real eye. Therefore, I played with makeup in my teen years to make both eyes appear to be the same. Now I could use the talent I developed to benefit others.

What intrigued me the most, however, had nothing to do with applying makeup — it was what happened when I removed the makeup of the woman I was working on.

Women came to the counter confidently to check in for their appointments. They asked a few questions, looked at the last woman I worked on and studied the available products and colors.

As I worked on each new client I put up a privacy screen or took the woman to a private room. As I cleansed her face, I could almost see each woman cower and glance warily around — even if we were alone. Apologies were made for untweezed eyebrows and imperfections of her skin. Many seemed fearful and anxious. They wanted me to know that they did not look this way.

I reassured each woman she was beautiful by quickly pointing out her assets. "You have beautiful eyes" or "What a great lip line." As the makeup went back on, each woman's confidence returned layer by layer. She felt safe again, asking me questions like, "How did you do that?" or "Where do I stop my liner?" Soon we were the best of friends.

Women often apologized for being so nervous, bought a large supply of makeup and skin care products, and left with renewed confidence.

It pleased me when a client left happy, but I was nevertheless disturbed that a woman would feel so vulnerable and unattractive without her makeup. It was almost as if I had uncovered something she was ashamed of, something she felt she should hide — her face.

Who Sets the Standard?

Perhaps you feel the same way. You may defend your position by reasoning that all women feel this way! This may be true — but should they? You are not what you see!

We have compared ourselves to a standard of perfection — one that always finds us wanting. It is the standard we find in the checkout line in the grocery store as we glance at the women on the covers of the fashion or fitness magazines. It is the one manufactured (and I do mean manufactured) by Hollywood. It is the standard set by those who labor for that which perishes. Their entire lives are centered on maintaining an image or an appearance.

By this standard, youth and folly are exalted while age and wisdom are despised. This is expected in the world, but I am not addressing the world right now. I'm talking to the church. We have allowed the world to set the pace and direct our taste. The world's system measures from the outside in while God measures from the inside out. The world loves appearances and hates the truth. God loves the truth and hates deceptive appearances.

Living Under the Influence

The women of Israel had come under the influence of the culture of their day. They allowed the culture around them to dictate the measure of a woman. They adorned themselves in the manner of the gentiles with each accessory designed to draw attention to them.

> Moreover, the Lord said, Because the daughters of Zion are haughty and walk with outstretched necks and with undisciplined (flirtatious and alluring) eyes, tripping along with mincing and affected gait, and making a tinkling noise with [the anklets on] their feet, Therefore the Lord will smite with a scab the crown of the heads of the daughters of Zion [making them bald], and the Lord will cause them to be [taken as captives and to suffer the indignity of being] stripped naked. In that day the Lord will take away the finery (Is. 3:16-18, AMP).

Isaiah continued to describe in detail all the finery that would be stripped away, everything from jewelry to hand mirrors, robes to undergarments, headbands to handbags. Sound familiar? Then he concluded:

And it shall come to pass that instead of the sweet odor of spices there shall be the stench of rottenness; and instead of a girdle, a rope; and instead of well-set hair, baldness; and instead of a rich robe, a girding of sackcloth; and searing [of captives by the scorching heat] instead of beauty (Is. 3:24).

Eventually the influence of their culture led the Israelites into bondage and captivity. They lost all the beauty they had taken such pains to create and all the accessories they had used to accent it.

Camel Queens

These women were a far cry from Rebekah who was drawing water from a well when she won a beauty contest and her prince.

And the girl was very beautiful and attractive, chaste and modest, and unmarried. And she went down to the well, filled her water jar, and came up (Gen. 24:16, AMP).

Rebekah was not adorned with costly apparel that drew attention to herself. How glamorous do you doll up for fetching water in the desert? She was adorned with good works. She was busy serving her family, and when she met a stranger she extended him hospitality.

After she had given him a drink, she said, "I'll draw water for your camels too, until they have finished drinking." So she quickly emptied her jar into the trough, ran back to the well to draw more water, and drew enough for all his camels. Without saying a word, the man watched her closely to learn whether or not the Lord had made his journey successful. When the camels had finished drinking, the man took out a gold nose ring weighing a beka and two gold bracelets weighing ten shekels (Gen. 24:19-22).

Her service won her adornment. She had not labored for the ring or bracelets. She had no idea these would be given to her. She labored because she was a servant.

Likewise, our good works bring us adornment as well as God's provision. It is interesting to note that Rebekah was given some of the same things that were later snatched away from the daughters of Zion. Jewelry was not the issue. Motive was. The daughters of Zion were too proud to serve. They spent their strength and wealth adorning and serving themselves instead of serving others. When calamity hit they were left without covering or provision.

God is not telling us to throw away our makeup and jewelry. I wear makeup and jewelry, but it is not what I labor for. The important thing is how you spend your strength and how you measure your worth. What do you allow to influence your life?

Do you adorn the hidden with the same zeal as you adorn the outward? If we are honest, most of us will admit we do not. We dress up our outward selves to the neglect of the inward. Others dress their outward to conceal their inward condition:

> You say, "I am rich; I have acquired wealth and do not need a thing." But you do not realize that you are wretched, pitiful, poor, blind and naked (Rev. 3:17).

We need to stop trying to conceal our inward conditions and instead allow God to heal us. He already knows our true conditions, yet He loves us. Untangle yourselves from the superficial and embrace the supernatural. It is urgent that we consecrate and separate ourselves, not by rending natural garments, but by tearing the hidden veil from our hearts.

> Rend your heart
>   and not your garments.
> Return to the Lord your God,
>   for he is gracious and compassionate,
> slow to anger and abounding in love,
>   and he relents from sending calamity (Joel 2:13).

As we lay down our desires
and rights, we hide ourselves
under the wings of His will.

8

Desert Daughters

When God refers to marriage His reference is not limited to or defined by our frail cultural perception.

"For your Maker is your husband —
   the Lord Almighty is his name —
the Holy One of Israel is your Redeemer;
   he is called the God of all the earth.
The Lord will call you back
   as if you were a wife deserted and distressed in
   spirit —
a wife who married young,
   only to be rejected," says your God.
"For a brief moment I abandoned you,
   but with deep compassion I will bring you
   back" (Is. 54:5-7).

Single or married, male or female, this promise stands as a covenant for every believer. God describes Himself as a Husband to an unfaithful wife whom He had put away in His anger, only to forgive, restore and draw once more to Himself.

He uses vivid and emotionally charged analogies to describe His relationship with His beloved Israel. But these analogies describe not only Israel the nation, they extend to spiritual Israel — the children of promise.

Our Marriage Covenant

This relationship is described in the New Testament with this comparison:

> For this reason a man will leave his father and mother and be united to his wife, and the two will become one flesh. This is a profound mystery — but I am talking about Christ and the church (Eph. 5:31-32).

If you as a believer are part of the church, this is your marriage covenant. Its principles, promises and provisions apply to you. They stand readily available for the single or married man or woman, Jew or gentile. In Romans the strength of this new covenant is illustrated:

> Do you not know, brothers — for I am speaking to men who know the law — that the law has authority over a man only as long as he lives? For example, by law a married woman is bound to her husband as long as he is alive, but if her husband dies, she is released from the law of marriage. So then, if she marries another man while her husband is still alive, she is called an adulteress. But if her husband dies, she is released from that law and is not an adulteress, even though she marries another man.

So, my brothers, you also died to the law through the body of Christ, that you might belong to another, to him who was raised from the dead, in order that we might bear fruit to God (Rom. 7:1-4).

We belong to another. Our old husband was the law of sin and death; our new Husband is Christ. We have died to the old in order to be free to embrace the new. Notice this higher spiritual application is illustrated and explained by a lower natural one. The application of the natural to explain the spiritual does not negate the laws of the natural; it validates them. The deeper spiritual significance undergirds and upholds the laws of nature.

Therefore, the recognition of your Maker as your Husband does not negate the natural law of marriage. It supersedes and surrounds the lesser with the supernatural protection and provision of the greater. The recognition and application of this truth brings the revelation of marriage and its purpose. It is divinely rooted in companionship with God. A man, Adam, and his wife, Eve, exist in union as one with their Creator. This is God's divine plan.

I have spoken in natural terms to explain the supernatural. Later in this book I will talk more about natural marriages. For now I want to move from the natural to the spiritual.

From this point forward in this chapter, I am not addressing the natural issue of being single or married. I am speaking of the relationship between God and the believer.

If we allow Him to do so, the Holy Spirit will reveal God as our Husband. He is worthy of our trust and His Word is worthy of our obedience. I pray you will study the scriptures in this chapter as though you were reading them for the first time.

Ageless Beauty

God used women to describe His bride and His church.

Therefore, I believe God's instructions to women hold keys for all believers.

> Let not yours be the [merely] external adorning with [elaborate] interweaving and knotting of the hair, the wearing of jewelry, or changes of clothes; But let it be the inward adorning and beauty of the hidden person of the heart, with the incorrupt-ible and unfading charm of a gentle and peaceful spirit, which [is not anxious or wrought up, but] is very precious in the sight of God (1 Pet. 3:3-4, AMP).

Notice it is precious to God when we trust Him. He sees the inner beauty others may miss. It never ages, fades or becomes corrupt. It is timeless and priceless. God treasures it. He guards and protects what is precious and valuable to Him.

> For it was thus that the pious women of old who hoped in God were (accustomed) to beautify them-selves and were submissive to their husbands — adapting themselves to them as themselves sec-ondary and dependent upon them (1 Pet. 3:5, AMP).

We are beautified with fadeless, ageless beauty when we submit and adapt our will to God's. As we lay down our desires and rights, we hide ourselves under the wings of His will. Here is an application of God's ageless beauty:

> It was thus that Sarah obeyed Abraham [following his guidance and acknowledging his headship over her by] calling him lord (master, leader, authority) (1 Pet. 3:6a, AMP).

When Sarah and Abraham traveled to foreign nations, Abraham was afraid for his personal safety because of Sarah's beauty. She was so beautiful that kings placed her in their harems, not when she was young, but when she was in her seventies or eighties. Abram told Sarai:

> "Say you are my sister, so that I will be treated well for your sake and my life will be spared because of you."
>
> When Abram came to Egypt, the Egyptians saw that she was a very beautiful woman. And when Pharaoh's officials saw her, they praised her to Pharaoh, and she was taken into his palace (Gen. 12:13-15).

> And Abimelech asked Abraham, "What was your reason for doing this?" Abraham replied, "I said to myself, 'There is surely no fear of God in this place, and they will kill me because of my wife'" (Gen. 20:10-11).

God protected Sarah even when her husband placed his safety above hers. God moved into the supernatural realm to protect her from the kings that had taken her into their harems. God did this because she was a precious treasure to Him. We are to follow her example by acknowledging and submitting to God's guidance and His headship over us.

> And you are now her true daughters if you do right and let nothing terrify you [not giving way to hysterical fears or letting anxieties unnerve you] (1 Pet. 3:6b, AMP).

Sarah had no natural daughters. But this promise states we can be her true daughters. I believe we are the daughters of promise, the daughters of a free woman, when we behave like our mother, Sarah. This means we do what we know to be right, not yielding to our hysterical fears and not allowing worry to steal our courage.

Sarah was a free woman. She was esteemed and honored because she esteemed and honored God and her husband. Hagar, on the other hand, was a slave woman, a captive who despised her mistress, Sarah. Hagar's offspring, Ishmael, followed his mother's pattern and mocked Isaac. Sarah understood there had to be a separation of the slave from the free.

> Get rid of the slave woman and her son, for the slave woman's son will never share in the inheritance with the free woman's son (Gal. 4:30).

The slave woman's son was not the only one denied a share of the inheritance. The slave woman was cast out from her inheritance also. Both the free woman and the slave woman had the same husband. They both had sons. Yet their relationship with Abraham was very different. Hagar represented the flesh and its bondage. Sarah represented the free and the promise. Galatians describes it this way:

> His son by the slave woman was born in the ordinary way; but his son by the free woman was born as the result of a promise.
>
> These things may be taken figuratively, for the women represent two covenants. One covenant is from Mount Sinai and bears children who are to be slaves: This is Hagar. Now Hagar stands for Mount Sinai in Arabia and corresponds to the present city of Jerusalem, because she is in slavery with her children. But the Jerusalem that is above is free, and she is our mother (Gal. 4:23-26).

There it is again — the promise of descendants from Sarah. Sarah's beauty was incorruptible, not only when she was young, but when she was old! She was a natural foreshadowing of the ageless, fadeless beauty found in Christ.

Sarah's Beauty Regimen

It is obvious from these accounts that Sarah was a woman of exceptional beauty. So let's see what her beauty regimen consisted of.

1. She left all that was comfortable and familiar.

2. She followed her husband to a strange land.

3. She lived in a tent in the desert.

4. She trusted God and did not fear or worry.

This was not the life of a pampered queen in a palace. It was a life of constant transition and faith. She would settle (if you call living in a tent "settling") in one place for a while, then travel across the desert to another. She was always waiting for the fulfillment of God's promise and trusting the guidance of her husband. She honored and obeyed her husband, and he honored and obeyed God. There is no record that she complained. She never looked back at what she left behind. Abraham, the father of faith, and his princess, Sarah, are an example and pattern of Christ and His bride, the church.

We are called to adapt ourselves as dependent and secondary to Christ. He is our Head, and all who believe are subject to His lordship, leadership and authority. But we have no reason to fear. He is our Maker-Husband. He has forged us with His love.

In the next chapter I want to look at the natural application of these truths to the marriage covenant.

When we feel out of control,
we try to control anything
that is within our power.

9

In Control and Hating It

The year was 1987, and I was stressed out, desperately attempting to be a professional employee, perfect mother and wife. My firstborn son was not quite a year old. I was still nursing, which required pumping my milk at work and spending lunch hours at the caregiver's home. I was adamant that all his baby food be prepared with natural, organic fruits and vegetables, so I made it all.

My demanding work schedule even extended into my weekends. I faced both professional and personal challenges at the office. Through it all I tried to look and act perfect. I was careful not to let on that I was crumbling under the weight of the pressures and demands placed upon me. To accomplish this I maintained a rigid schedule, and I became obsessed with control.

Notice I did not mention my husband. There is a reason: I considered him to be the very lowest on my list of priorities. I justified my attitude by reasoning that he was an adult and could fend for himself. After all, these other areas demanded my attention and expertise.

Yet there was an even deeper reason for my lack of attention. John and I had learned to coexist in our separate worlds. When those worlds occasionally collided, they exploded with anger and careless words.

At that time I worked more hours than John and was solely responsible for the care of our child. I felt John was unresponsive and insensitive to my needs and the demands upon my life. I felt he did not carry his share. So I nagged, criticized and belittled him in what appeared to be a futile attempt to change him.

John was not the man he is now. He was in a very uncomfortable time of transition, determined to find and fulfill God's purpose and design for his life. This pursuit consumed him to the neglect of all else. It seemed the more he strove to find God's direction, the more it eluded him. John became uncertain and unsure of himself. He hoped for this prospect or that, only to be disappointed.

I too was disappointed and discouraged. I was beginning to wonder if John could even hear from God. I was tired of working full time. I wanted to be home with my son, but I was afraid to quit. Frustrated, I had resigned myself to cynicism, developing an I'll-believe-it-when-I-see-it attitude.

When John would excitedly share with me what he believed God had shown him, I sighed and rolled my eyes. *Here we go again*, I thought. I became very quick and careless with my opinions. I was under the mistaken impression that God had put John and I together because I was so wise (in my own eyes, of course) and could counsel John. I saw it as my endless duty to share my critical wisdom and insight with him.

Often I was correct in my assessment, which I was quick to bring to John's attention. "See, I told you!" I gloated. I thought this revelation would cause John to realize the accuracy of my counsel and draw him closer to me. But it had just the opposite effect. I was a know-it-all who made John feel like a failure.

Sensing that his own wife did not believe in him, he pulled away from me. He soon took counsel outside our marriage. Both of us withdrew from each other.

I continued to work full time while John worked part time. He prayed for hours, fasted, talked to his friends and played golf. At the same time I was stressed and worried over insurance benefits and our financial provision. I resented his lack of involvement. I blamed him for all the pressure I felt. My employer was in the midst of a huge lay-off, and I feared for my position. Worry and stress became a way of life for me.

Crisis Management

The fact is we never actually faced a crisis. I was just planning ahead and worrying in advance for any future one. Soon my fears and anxieties overwhelmed me. I wanted John to feel some of the pressure I was experiencing.

But no matter how hard I tried to persuade John to worry with me, he would not. He declared that God had everything under control. I was certain God was not in control. In my eyes, I was holding things together, and I could feel my grip slipping. My response was to panic. I was convinced that John was in denial. "What if I lose my job?" I'd probe. "We will have no insurance benefits!"

"Are you about to lose your job?" John would ask.

"No! Of course not!" I countered. "But what if I did? Do you have a plan?"

"God will have one if that should happen," John answered calmly. "Lisa, just let go of this and surrender it to God."

Never! I would think. *If I'm not taking care of all this it won't get done.*

I felt so out of control that I tried to control everything that was within my power. I took it upon myself to remind John to do everything. I would nag him about the garbage only to find it sitting in the kitchen when I came home from work.

I felt it extremely important to remain responsible, and this meant worrying about everything. Since John was not willing to join me, I worried for the both of us. I was tormented because I measured our future and financial security by my limited ability to provide.

Sometimes my fears became so extreme and real, I'd wake John from a sound sleep to inform him that I was carrying much more than my fair share of stress. "If you would only pay attention to these things, I'd be able to rest," I complained. But he would not concede. He again suggested I give my heaviest cares to God and go to sleep. But I didn't want to give them to God. I wanted to give them to John!

On paper my reasoning sounds absurd, but it seemed very logical and sound at the time. My imagined fears were no less real to me than if they had actually happened. Some of you can laugh at me, while others may see yourself in my frantic panic.

Giving Up the Yoke

Worry is both a noun and a verb. In its verb form it means "to harass, vex, irritate, plague and torment." I was definitely experiencing all of the above. I was tormented, so, in turn, I tormented. Worry is unbelief in action and it is fueled by fear.

I was constantly plagued by fear while worry choked the Word of God from my life. My mind was never at rest but constantly scrambling as I mentally ran the gauntlet of every imaginable crisis.

Needless to say, it had been a long time since I had known any type of rest or peace. Tension was my constant companion, and complaining and nagging my main form of communication. I was physically exhausted yet unable to rest. Even in my sleep I wrestled with my fear and worries.

I thought perhaps I just needed to wind down before I went to bed. So with visions of Calgon, I tried to relax by taking a bath or shower before I retired. In the tub I would submerge myself until only my nose remained above water. That way I could still breathe, but I did not have to see or hear anything. But even under water you cannot run from what is inside your mind. On other nights I'd shower until there was no hot water left, but to no avail. I still couldn't escape the internal and external pressures that weighed upon me.

Tension gripped my shoulders and neck like a taskmaster. I experienced the hopeless frustration of feeling responsible for something I did not have the authority to change. My load was too heavy because it was not mine to bear.

One night while in the shower I complained to God instead of John about this heavy load. I whined and explained how overwhelmed I felt because I couldn't relinquish any of my burden to John. After all, if he didn't even remember the garbage, how could I trust him with anything more important? I wrestled back and forth, justifying why I could not relinquish control.

"Lisa, do you think John is a good leader?" the Lord gently asked me.

"No, I do not!" I asserted. "I don't trust him!"

"Lisa, you don't have to trust John," He replied. "You only have to trust Me. You don't think John is doing a very good job as the head of this home. You feel that you can do better. The tension and unrest you're experiencing is the weight and pressure of being the head of a household. It's a yoke to you, but a mantle to John. Lay it down, Lisa."

Immediately I saw it! The headship of our home was

oppressive to me because it was not my position to fill. It would not be oppressive to John because God had anointed him as the head of the home. I recognized how I had jockeyed and fought for the lead position in our home. I realized how critical and faultfinding I had become. I had torn down my husband instead of building him up and believing in him. He, in turn, had relinquished his position of authority to me, and I had made a mess of it.

Broken, I turned off the shower and grabbed a towel. Immediately I found John in our bedroom. I wept and apologized for all my belittling and nagging, solemnly promising, "John, I will get behind you and support you. I believe in you."

At the time I was not certain what I was supporting or believing in. I only knew John needed this support more than I needed all the details of what and why. I recognized that everything was terribly out of order in our home. I wanted God to order the chaos I had created. In turn John also apologized for not leading and for withdrawing from me. We struck a covenant to love, support and draw from each other.

That night I thought I was dying to the hope of ever seeing my desires and needs provided for, but I did not care. For the first time in years I slept and actually found rest. My yoke of bondage had been removed.

Yokes and Mantles

To understand what had transpired it is important to know the meaning of yoke.[1] A yoke symbolizes oppression due to heavy responsibility, duty or sin. It represents a burden so great you cannot escape it but are controlled by it. Its bearer has no authority over it; the yoke is the mas-

---

1. *Nelson's Illustrated Bible Dictionary* (Nashville, Tenn.: Thomas Nelson, 1986), s.v. tools of the Bible. Also *The New Smith's Bible Dictionary* (Garden City, N.Y.: Doubleday and Co., 1966), s.v. yoke.

ter. It signifies slavery or servitude. The phrase "to break a yoke" means to secure your freedom.

We are under a yoke of bondage any time we carry what God never intended for us to bear. This is not limited to marriage. Often as I minister I can discern when a person is under oppression, depression and fear. Beyond the recognition of their outward effects, I can also sense the yoke's weight and strain on their shoulders. In the spirit I can see the person bent under a weight that is too heavy for him or her to carry. The person struggles and labors against it, but the yoke always oppresses him or her in the end. The yoke is not the person's to carry. This principle is not limited to natural marriage, but it includes anything we carry that we were not meant to carry.

On the other hand a mantle represents protection, warmth, covering and position.[2] It was designed to be totally nonrestrictive, a sleeveless cloak worn over other garments. It was large enough to carry and conceal things within its folds. At night it was used as a bed covering.

A mantle's detail and ornamentation represented social standing or position. Samuel's mantle was fashioned by his mother as a miniature of the priestly garment. Joseph's mantle incorporated many colors, calling attention to him and exalting him above his brothers. Isaiah and John the Baptist wore mantles of animal skin, signifying their unique and similar prophetic callings.

A mantle covers our nakedness, conceals our faults, carries supplies and announces our authority or position to those around us.

I had been yoked, and John had been dismantled. No wonder we were in a mess! When I submitted to God's established order for the household, my yoke was broken and John was cloaked in God's mantle of leadership. I was

---

2. *Nelson's,* s.v. dress of the Bible. *Smith's,* s.v. mantle.

covered also, for the mantle spread to cover and protect me and all persons under John's care. When we are in proper submission to Christ, we are covered and cloaked in all that His mantle represents.

This principle applies to everyone — woman or man, married or single. Christ is your priest, protection and provision. Dare to trust Him and the authority structure He has established. He is our Husband and Advocate with the Father.

Construction Zone

At first it was very difficult for me to relinquish control. But all the events of that last year had caused me to realize I had never really been in control — I had been fighting God's control.

As I surveyed the mess I had created, I knew I could no longer trust myself. It was time to let God's wisdom prevail. It was time to rebuild what had been torn asunder.

> The wise woman builds her house, but with her own hands the foolish one tears hers down (Prov. 14:1).

By foolishly trying to build security and structure with my own hands I had inadvertently torn it down. I had demolished God's order. Unless God builds the house you labor in vain (Ps. 127:1). It was glaringly apparent that all my worry and stress had been wasteful and destructive to both my marriage and my health.

Often when we are frustrated with the progress of God's process in our lives or in the lives of those around us, we decide to help out. But instead of building, we end up tearing down the walls of protection God provided for our relationships. This demolition occurs through the wrecking ball of criticism, belittling, nagging and complaining.

In a desperate attempt to hold it all together I watched it slip from my hands. I grasped and clutched, only to open my arms and find them empty. I was so thankful that God had exposed my folly before it was too late.

So often we are afraid to trust God to build our home. So we take out our blueprints and start construction. When we run up against immovable walls, faulty foundations and depleted resources, we cry out for help!

Perhaps you're at just such a place. God is waiting. He will step out of the shadows where He has patiently watched your frantic project. We have His gracious assurance that His plan is best. His blueprint includes meeting not only our needs, but even our deepest unspoken desires.

When I no longer felt responsible to affect changes in John, I felt free to apply that same energy toward loving him. I could enjoy him again. I was so thankful for God's mercy that I was quick to forgive what I perceived as shortcomings in John. I began to watch for the good, not the bad. Though none of our outward circumstances changed, the pressures were gone. I continued to work full time, but now it was different. I did not view myself as the source and John as the problem. I knew God was our source and the answer.

John was different too. He was more settled and content. He no longer felt he had to earn my respect because I respected the position God had given him in our home. In turn he was more considerate. It was not unusual for John to straighten the house or have dinner ready when I got home from work. He even bought dishes and a washer and dryer as a surprise for me.

New Man

I watched my husband go from a boy to a man of the Spirit. There was a new boldness, decisiveness and authority on his life. God answered every one of my prayers and exceeded my expectations. I respect my husband as a man of God, not just because I am commanded to honor and respect him, but because I believe with all my heart he is a man of God. I personally have experienced more peace, authority, protection and anointing on my life since I relinquished control and threw aside my yoke. John is my best friend. He is my companion and a gift from God.

Where rampant confusion had reigned, faith, peace and love now ruled. We were actually content. We enjoyed each other and the precious son God had given us. It was in this atmosphere that God's promotion for John came. There was no striving or struggling this time. When God's door opened it was clear and obvious. We were both amazed at how fast God set everything in order. God could trust us now because we were in agreement. The two were one.

Perhaps some of you have prayed for your husband to change. Release this burden to your Husband-Maker. It is too much for you to bear.

God's New Order

It is important to remember we are the family of God. He is our Father and we are His children. Before there ever was a church as we know it there was the family. God's plan for our households is better than ours — His provides protection, provision, peace and pleasure. It is a good plan because He is a good God.

We are witnessing this restoration in men. God is turning their hearts back to Him. Because God is a Father, He is reminding them of their roles as husbands and fathers. When God leads He wants the men to follow. He wants them to be strong.

For too long women have been blamed for the weakness of men. The religious philosophy was: If the women will back down the men will be strong. The truth is that weak women don't make strong men. God makes strong men.

God also makes strong women. God never intended for women to restore their men. He will restore them. It is important that we are in position to receive the blessing of this process.

God is preparing and commissioning men to lead their homes as priests, not lords. They will not be perfect priests. They will make mistakes. But are we willing to follow? God is preparing a priesthood to set His house in order. He is anointing them with hearts set apart to Him. This anointing will give men hearts for their families.

It is the answer to our prayers, but are we ready? Most likely God will not do this in the manner we expect or pray He will. For a season it may be uncomfortable and unfamiliar, but it will eventually bring refreshing and renewal. God will show Himself sovereign and receive all the glory. His plan will produce our heart's desire.

A Kingdom in Transition

We find just such a transition in the history of the nation of Israel. God had anointed David to be king in Saul's stead. Saul had turned from the counsel of the Lord, and God rejected him as king. God replaced Saul with David, a man after His own heart.

David had been joined with the house of Saul by his marriage to Michal, Saul's daughter. David had won her hand in marriage when he killed the giant, Goliath. Michal would come to embody the conflict between Saul and David's kingdoms.

During Saul's reign the ark of the covenant had not been restored to God's temple. When David became king he brought the ark back to Jerusalem. In celebration of its return David lost all awareness of himself. Overwhelmed by God's goodness and mercy he took off his outer garments and danced before the Lord and all of Israel.

But not everyone was as happy as David. Michal watched

this display of worship from her upper window.

> And when she saw King David leaping and danc-
> ing before the Lord, she despised him in her heart
> (2 Sam. 6:16).

Michal was not ready to embrace this freedom. She failed to realize it was God who had removed her father and enthroned her husband. She wanted to cling to the old order of her father's house. After all, she was royalty, a descendent of the first king of Israel. Draped in pride, she despised David's humility and exposure. She tried to humiliate him in front of his elders.

> When David returned home to bless his house-
> hold, Michal daughter of Saul came out to meet
> him and said, "How the king of Israel has distin-
> guished himself today, disrobing in the sight of the
> slave girls of his servants as any vulgar fellow
> would!" (2 Sam. 6:20).

Even though he was her husband and the king, she did not honor him. Perhaps she resented his freedom when she felt so bound.

As is often true, David found the greatest resistance within his own house. Michal had hoped David's love for her would allow her to control him. But David's love for God exceeded any desire he had for a position of honor in his home or kingdom.

> David said to Michal, "It was before the Lord, who
> chose me rather than your father or anyone from
> his house when he appointed me ruler over the
> Lord's people Israel—I will celebrate before the
> Lord. I will become even more undignified than
> this, and I will be humiliated in my own eyes. But

by these slave girls you spoke of, I will be held in honor."

And Michal daughter of Saul had no children to the day of her death (2 Sam. 6:21-23).

Michal's plan backfired. She had misused her position when she tried to manipulate David's love for her. She not only lost the love and favor of her husband, but the chance for any children. She was barren for the rest of her life. She had lost the heart of the man she tried to control.

David, however, denied himself the honor of man and the affection of his wife to embrace the honor of God.

This tragedy holds an important lesson. We must not spurn the leadership God has established in our lives. We should not mock them (leaders) when they come to bless us in a manner or method we are not accustomed to. They may not worship or lead the way we think they should. Remember, when God takes control of a leader, it is for the benefit and protection of all those under that leader's care.

This principle is not confined to marriage; it represents the authority of Christ and His church. It symbolizes the transition from the old to the new, from controlling to letting go. The choice is ours. Will we choose to enjoy the blessings of renewal or mock it from the sidelines, bitter and barren?

Bringing It Home

Let us not confine this principle to male/female relationships. This applies to any area where we are faced with a decision to hang on to the old or go on to the new. It's about leaving the comfortable and moving to the unexpected.

Think about the past year of your life. Would you say, as I did, that you have been stressed out? Are you burning yourself to the ground trying to stay in control of areas that

God never meant for you to shoulder? Are you in control—and hating it?

Ask God to show you the difference between a yoke and a mantle. Remember that a yoke enslaves you by making you responsible for something that is not your responsibility and not under your control. A mantle, on the other hand, rests on you when you operate in the authority and anointing that God has ordained for you.

God taught me this principle in the context of my marriage. But it applies much further than that. Any responsibility you take up that God did not ordain for you will put you in a yoke. However, when God gives you a calling to fulfill, His mantle of anointing will help you to accomplish it.

Pray with me:

> God,
>
> I ask You to show me any yokes that have encumbered me. Help me to lay them aside. Lord, show me the calling that You have for my life right now. I pray for the mantle of anointing that will help me to fulfill it. Lord, help me rebuild any areas that I have torn down by not following You, amen.

———————————

Love challenges us to doubt
what we can see and
believe what we cannot.

———————————

10

Fear: The Battle for Your Mind

Why would anyone despise God's order in their life? Why would they struggle to hold on when they should let go? Why would they want to retain and not relinquish control? Why? Because they are afraid.

Fear is an insidious force. It causes reason and wisdom to escape us. It drives and compels, pushing us to the brink of unbelief. To overcome fear we must know its nature. Fear is not a mental state of mind or a bad attitude. It is a spirit.

> For God has not given us a spirit of fear, but of power and of love and of a sound mind (2 Tim. 1:7, NKJV).

Fear is a spirit. It is not from God. It is sent by the enemy to torment our souls and defile our human spirits. Fear comes to steal our power, love and soundness of mind. As a spiritual force, fear must be confronted spiritually.

Battling for Power

Fear is only empowered to the degree we yield to its deception. Fear steals our power by tricking us into believing its lies. Imaginary fears can become real if we believe in them. Even the most unfounded ones can alter the course of our lives and in turn change our destinies.

The destination for the children of Israel was the promised land, but they forsook God's promises to embrace their fears. They placed their faith in their fears. In doing this they chose the devil's lies over God's truth.

God said:

> I have come down to rescue them from the hand of the Egyptians and to bring them up out of that land into a good and spacious land, a land flowing with milk and honey...See, I am sending an angel ahead of you to guard you along the way and to bring you to the place I have prepared (Ex. 3:8; 23:20).

Fear said:

> We can't attack those people; they are stronger than we are...They spread among the Israelites a bad report...They said, "The land we explored devours those living in it. All the people we saw there are of great size...We seemed like grasshoppers in our own eyes, and we looked the same to them" (Num. 13:31-33).

They believed:

> Why is the Lord bringing us to this land only to let us fall by the sword? Our wives and children will be taken as plunder. Wouldn't it be better for us to go back to Egypt? (Num. 14:3).

When they chose fear's lie over God's truth, they forfeited their power to possess the promised land God had already given them. Instead of inheriting the promises, they inherited their fears.

> As surely as I live, declares the Lord, I will do to you the very things I heard you say: In this desert your bodies will fall — every one of you twenty years old or more...who has grumbled against me. Not one of you will enter the land I swore with uplifted hand to make your home, except Caleb son of Jephunneh and Joshua son of Nun. As for your children that you said would be taken as plunder, I will bring them in to enjoy the land you have rejected...Your children will be shepherds here for forty years, suffering for your unfaithfulness, until the last of your bodies lies in the desert (Num. 14:28-33).

God never planned for a generation of Israelites to die as they wandered the wilderness. His plan was to rescue them from the Egyptians and bring them, escorted by an angel, to a good land.

Fear had so twisted and perverted their spiritual perception of God that the Israelites imagined God had tricked them. They believed He had delivered them from Egyptian oppression in order to turn them over to be slaughtered by the heathen nations of Canaan.

Their logic sounds ridiculous, doesn't it? Yet how often do we unknowingly succumb to the same sort of unreasonable fears? Fear causes us to shrink back into doubt and unbelief.

Fear is after our faith. It wants us to place our faith in it and not in the promise of God. Our faith will always work — but will it work *for* us or *against* us?

The Bible says that God gives each of us a measure of

faith (Rom. 12:3). We are to be stewards of this faith. God wants us to use our faith to be conformed to the image of His Son. However, the enemy wants to use it against us and conform us to a different image. Don't turn the power of faith over to the enemy of God.

Fighting for Love

Fear is after your love because the enemy knows that love protects the believer from fear.

> God is love. Whoever lives in love lives in God, and God in him...There is no fear in love (1 John 4:16,18).

There is no greater protection afforded you than to live in God's love. It is here that you are hidden and inaccessible to the enemy.

The love of God drives out or casts out fear. This description again confirms that fear is a spiritual force that must be dealt with spiritually. (We are called to cast out spirits and deny our flesh. We cannot deny a spirit and cast out your flesh, even though some of us have tried.)

The very nature of love opposes the nature of fear. Love's nature is described by the following verses:

> Love is patient, love is kind. It does not envy, it does not boast, it is not proud. It is not rude, it is not self-seeking, it is not easily angered, it keeps no record of wrongs. Love does not delight in evil but rejoices with the truth. It always protects, always trusts, always hopes, always perseveres (1 Cor. 13:4-7).

We can go through the above list and insert the opposite attributes of fear. Fear is impatient, mean, jealous, boastful, proud, rude, self-seeking and easily angered. It keeps a record of wrongs. It delights when the bad it predicted happens. It never protects, trusts, hopes or perseveres.

Fear is the opposite of love. Love and fear both operate from belief in the unseen. Love challenges us to doubt what we see and believe what we cannot. Fear urges us to believe what is seen while doubting the unseen. Fear displaces love and love casts out fear. Fear is the spiritual force that is in direct opposition to God's love and protection in our lives.

Jesus has already conquered the greatest fear any of us will face — the fear of death. As our High Priest He was moved with compassion by our weaknesses and understood not only the fear of death, but all our fears. By victoriously facing our greatest fear (death), He conquered all lesser fears and their bondage.

> Since the children have flesh and blood, he too shared in their humanity so that by his death he might destroy him who holds the power of death — that is, the devil — and free those who all their lives were held in slavery by their fear of death (Heb. 2:14-15).

Fear will hold you in slavery if you allow it. Jesus triumphed over every grip of fear when He laid down His life on the cross.

> Greater love has no one than this, that he lay down his life for his friends (John 15:13).

Jesus laid down His life out of His love for us. Jesus conquered the fear that had mastered Adam. The fear of death had ruled since Adam's transgression in the garden. It was Adam's desire to be like God which caused him to transgress.

Fear in the Garden

God carefully warned Adam when He commanded the man:

> You must not eat from the tree of the knowledge of good and evil, for when you eat of it you will surely die (Gen. 2:17).

The knowledge of good and evil is the law of sin and death. God wanted Adam to remain in the liberty of His knowledge of God. Adam had gained this knowledge by loving and fellowshipping with God. He did not need the knowledge of good and evil to walk with God. Adam was already walking with God. Satan did not want Adam and Eve to remain free and alive under this law of liberty so he perverted God's warning of protection.

> "You will not surely die," the serpent said to the woman. "For God knows that when you eat of it your eyes will be opened, and you will be like God, knowing good and evil" (Gen. 3:4-5).

Adam knew God was life, and in Him there was no darkness or death. Satan made it sound as though God were intentionally deceiving Adam to prevent him from becoming like God. What Satan did was twofold; first, He undermined God by questioning His truthfulness and motives; second, He appealed to Adam's desire to be like God but not subject to Him. His underlying message was, "Why should you believe and obey God? He doesn't have your best interests in mind. Be the lord of yourself."

Adam and Eve believed this deception. They ate the fruit hoping it would provide the wisdom necessary to be their own masters. They reasoned that the more they were like God, the less they would be subject to Him.

But were they now *more* like God? Let's examine Adam's first reply to God after eating the fruit.

> I heard you in the garden, and I was afraid because I was naked; so I hid (Gen. 3:10).

If Adam and Eve had become more like God, why were they more afraid of Him, hiding from His presence?

Fear distorted Adam's perception of God. He became afraid of the very One who formed and breathed life into him. Adam feared his Creator because he had transgressed God's command.

Perfect love and fear cannot abide together so Adam had to leave the garden of God. The fear of judgment will always come between you and the presence of God.

Adam's transgression brought him under the law of sin and death. Adam choose the knowledge of good and evil (the law) over the knowledge of God (a love relationship by the Spirit). Adam wanted to be like God apart from God. Adam grasped for equality with God.

The second Adam, Jesus, was God and became man. He is our example:

> Your attitude should be the same as that of Christ Jesus: Who, being in very nature God, did not consider equality with God something to be grasped...he humbled himself and became obedient to death — even death on a cross! (Phil. 2:5-6,8).

Jesus lived His life under the rule and dominion of God His Father. He was not self-ruled. He refused to move independent of God. He thrived on obeying God (John 4:34). Through obedience Jesus reversed the law of sin and death and its dominion of fear.

Through Christ Jesus the law of the Spirit of life set
me free from the law of sin and death (Rom. 8:2).

We are therefore governed by the Spirit and not by the
law. Fear cannot wage its war in a heart submitted to and
directed by the love of God.

Now let's go on to why fear attacks your soundness of
mind.

A Sound Mind

Since fear is a spiritual force without form, it must inhabit
something to gain expression. It seeks to inhabit the
fortresses of the mind. The battle of fear is waged in our
minds.

One of Satan's battle strategies is to torment us with questions. Satan questioned Eve as to whether God really meant
what He had said. He was trying to undermine God and
make Him look like a liar.

Fear behaves the same way. It always questions, distorts
and undermines what God has said. *How do you know God
will do what He said? Maybe you misunderstood Him. God
really meant this? That promise does not apply to you.*

Fear wants you to compromise the integrity of the Word
of God. God has exalted His Word above His name (Ps.
138:2) so when we doubt His Word we doubt all that He is.
Fear wants us to doubt God's goodness, mercy, faithfulness,
holiness, power, glory and everything else that makes Him
God. Fear will try to misrepresent the nature and motive of
God by twisting His Word. This will cause us to doubt God,
and we do not trust or believe those we doubt.

Fear wants to convince us God did not mean what He
said or say what He meant. By undermining God's character and distorting His words, fear brings in confusion to
torment us. Confusion attacks the soundness, or wholeness,
of our minds.

Confusion divides our allegiance between God and self. This leaves us with a double mind. James 1:6-8 accurately describes this confusion:

> But when he asks, he must believe and not doubt, because he who doubts is like a wave of the sea, blown and tossed by the wind. That man should not think he will receive anything from the Lord; he is a double-minded man, unstable in all he does (James 1:6-8).

When we are confused we are unstable. Instability causes a person to waver and shift — not just in one area but in all he does. James said that if we doubt, we shouldn't think we'll receive anything from the Lord. James made this comment while asking for wisdom. So when we lose soundness or wholeness of mind, we lose the guidance of God. Uncertainty takes over. We don't know what to expect from God so we take matters into our own hands.

Fear mocks, *What will happen if you let go? Who will watch out for you?* Fear has torment (1 John 4:18) because it leads us to question, *What is going to happen to me?* Such questioning diverts your attention from God and back to ourselves. Fear encourages us to safeguard our well-being. It wants us to preserve ourselves.

Self preservation requires us to be self-centered, self-serving, selfish, self-willed and self-ruled. These attributes directly oppose God's directives for our lives and thus remove God's protection. The enemy wants us to serve in the kingdom of self. In this kingdom self rules, therefore self is our god.

Fight Back

Now that we've seen how fear attacks in the arenas of power, love and soundness of mind, let's look at how we can fight back against the strongholds of fear.

Author Francis Frangipane describes a stronghold in our mind as a "house of thoughts." Strongholds of fear are often constructed from the lies of the enemy and from debris left over from past hurt and abuse. These materials from past offenses are collected and used to construct walls to protect us from those we fear will hurt us. Fear instead of faith establishes the thought patterns through which all information is processed. Every thought is conformed to the image of fear and unbelief.

Our reasoning is distorted, and our soundness of mind is disturbed. This explains how we can say something to a person tormented by fear and that person will hear something entirely different. The words are heard, but the meaning is distorted. That is why God could say, "You will be ever hearing but never understanding" (Acts 28:26). They heard, but because of unbelief they could not perceive or understand the meaning of what they heard.

> The weapons we fight with are not the weapons of the world. On the contrary, they have divine power to demolish strongholds. We demolish arguments and every pretension that sets itself up against the knowledge of God, and we take captive every thought to make it obedient to Christ (2 Cor. 10:4-5).

God wants these strongholds demolished. Notice these arguments and pretensions set themselves up against or in opposition to the knowledge of God. Remember, the battle is in our minds. The enemy wants to set self in opposition to the knowledge of God. To combat this God wants every thought that wars against our minds to be taken hostage and conformed to the image of Christ (2 Cor. 10:5). That means we are to capture the messages of fear and unbelief and subject them to the truth of God's Word. Jesus is the

Word made flesh, so when we subject our thoughts to the Word we are subjecting them to Christ (John 1:1-3,14).

We are not to make our thoughts obedient to the law; the Bible says to make them obedient to Christ. The law has no power to tear down these strongholds. In fact, it helps with their construction.

> Once I was alive apart from law; but when the commandment came, sin sprang to life and I died. I found that the very commandment that was intended to bring life actually brought death. For sin, seizing the opportunity afforded by the commandment, deceived me, and through the commandment put me to death (Rom. 7:9-11).

> For what the law was powerless to do in that it was weakened by the sinful nature, God did by sending his own Son in the likeness of sinful man to be a sin offering. And so he condemned sin in sinful man...For you did not receive a spirit that makes you a slave again to fear, but you received the Spirit of sonship. And by him we cry, "Abba, Father" (Rom. 8:3,15).

We died to the rule of the law of sin and death when we were crucified with Christ. At that point we received the spirit of sonship. Instead of self ruling us, Christ became our king. Therefore we are subject to Him.

Under the law we were created in the image of our natural father Adam. But in the new and living law of life in Christ Jesus we are granted sonship with our Father God.

Renew Your Mind

Because we are under an aggressive onslaught from the enemy, we must also be aggressive in the protection of our minds. We must guard them diligently. This is accomplished by renewing our minds through the Word of God.

> Do not conform any longer to the pattern of this world, but be transformed by the renewing of your mind. Then you will be able to test and approve what God's will is — his good, pleasing and perfect will (Rom. 12:2).

Fear always casts doubt on us knowing the will of God, but we can know God's will through the transformation of our minds. If we are able to know His good, pleasing and perfect will, we will not be afraid to submit to it.

> The mind of sinful man is death, but the mind controlled by the Spirit is life and peace (Rom. 8:6).

God wants our minds controlled by His Spirit, not by the spirit of fear. Fear will keep us in constant restlessness and confusion. It does not want us to experience peace. Notice that the sinful, unbelieving mind leads to death, while God's Spirit leads us to the path of life and peace.

> You will keep in perfect peace him whose mind is steadfast, because he trusts in you (Is. 26:3).

God will do this because we trust Him and choose to believe that He meant what He said. We experience peace when we choose His faithfulness over fear.

Renewing our minds is more than just a knowledge of the Scriptures. It is trusting His goodness and faithfulness even when we don't understand how His Word will be accomplished in our lives. By believing what we don't see and understand, we mix His Word with faith. This is the only way God's Word becomes alive in us.

For we also have had the gospel preached to us, just as they did; but the message they heard was of no value to them, because those who heard did not combine it with faith (Heb. 4:1-2).

The knowledge of the gospel was of no value to the children of Israel wandering in the wilderness even though they were accompanied day and night by His presence, a cloud by day and a pillar of fire by night. We are warned that the same can happen to us if we are not careful.

To inherit God's promise of eternal life Jesus instructed:

Love the Lord your God with all your heart and with all your soul and with all your mind (Matt. 22:37).

In the next three chapters we will expose some specific fruits of fear — anger, gossip and self-neglect. We'll learn to identify the nature and motive behind each fruit so we can eliminate its influence on our lives.

As long as we justify
our anger or make excuses for it
we remain captive.

11

Escaping
Anger

I can't help it. It's just the way I am!" I don't know how many times I've used that one, but I do know what prompted me. That statement was usually hurled in justification of my anger. My excuses covered a wide range of topics:

- I'm Sicilian, Apache Indian, French and English.

- I'm about to start my period.

- I'm having my period.

- I'm pregnant.

- I'm postpartum.

- It's the way I was raised.

- I'm working full time and taking care of a baby.

- I'm stuck home with young children.

- I'm under a spiritual attack! (This one was especially useful since it absolved me of all responsibility.)

And the list went on. But the truth was, I had a problem with anger. Deep down I knew this but did not want to take the necessary steps to face it. I felt certain I could control any anger as long as all my circumstances and everyone around me cooperated by being perfect!

But my circumstances, mainly those involving my husband and children, were not cooperating. It is impossible for anyone to be perfect, and their human flaws served to magnify and point out mine.

If the heat turned up and I was under pressure, then what lurked under my surface became glaringly apparent. I would become consumed with anger and lash out at the ones I loved most.

At first it was just an occasional outburst, perhaps once every three months. Then it rapidly became a way of life. Oddly enough, the intensifying of my anger seemed to be the result of my own prayers.

A Surprising Answer to Prayer

On New Year's Eve of 1987, I wept and cried out to the Lord. I begged Him to take His coal and cleanse my lips. I declared the all-consuming fire was my heart's desire. I had hoped to experience a vision or dream, one in which an angel would visit me with a coal from the throne of heaven. But God had a very different process in mind to answer my prayer.

Truthfully, I prayed with a lot of religious pride and self-righteousness. I judged myself by my intentions and made excuses for my actions. But I judged everyone else by their actions and even dared to suppose I knew their motives. I was pure in my own eyes and critical of everyone else.

I had recently left Dallas and all that was comfortable and familiar to me so my husband could become a pastor. I smugly sat in the front row at church, nodding my head. In my own eyes I'd arrived.

I reasoned that God gave me this position of pastor's wife because His approval was on my life. He liked me just the way I was. I doubted that He could find a whole lot left that still needed to be changed in me. I prayed, not out of brokenness, but out of pride.

I was sadly mistaken. I was wrong to believe position or promotion was a sign of God's approval on my life. Wrong to think there was little left in need of change. Wrong to think my minor sacrifices earned me favor or righteousness.

Within a month of my prayer I found myself angrier than ever. For no apparent reason I would awake in the morning with all the signs of a volcano inside. All I could feel was the rumbling. Often I would warn my husband, "If you are smart you will not push me today." John would roll his eyes and challenge my announcement by daring to ask me what I was upset about. This would always frustrate me because I was never quite certain why I awakened on edge. So I usually blamed it on something vague or too ambiguous to solve or address. John then realized speaking to me would just be a waste of his time, so he sidestepped me that day.

Then my day would proceed, filled with all the normal interruptions and frustrations. But on those days the normal seemed unbearably magnified. I would slam cabinets and doors, huffing and puffing through our home like a steam engine. I'd cast a warning eye at anyone who even dared to cross me slightly.

Inevitably, something John did or said would set me off, and I would go on a rampage. I said all sorts of ugly things to my husband, things I later regretted. I reasoned that I had told him to leave me alone. It was not my fault; he had been forewarned. I believed I was under a demonic attack by a spirit of rage and therefore I was not responsible for my actions.

On one particular Saturday morning I awoke with another rumble of anger, and as the morning progressed, things went from bad to worse. I stomped and huffed around the house and verbally vented at John the majority of my grievances. Finally I was winding down as I stood in the laundry room unloading the dryer. John heard me slam the dryer door, and he ran in and caught me bent over the laundry basket. To my shock he gently picked me up, carried me out to the garage and locked me out of the house.

From inside the house he informed me, "You are not going to damage anything in this home by throwing a fit!"

The garage door was open and I was in no danger, but I was incensed that he had put me out in the garage like a dog or cat. I demanded that he open the door to the house.

"No!" John said.

"I'll go to the neighbors!" I bluffed.

"Go ahead," countered John.

I became even more frustrated, and decided I needed to break something to make me feel better. I picked up a hammer and began my search. I wanted to be certain that I did not break anything I'd be sorry to lose later when my wrath subsided.

We had recently moved and the garage was filled with boxes. Finally after nearly fifteen minutes I found my victim in the corner — the Weber grill. Raising my hammer I dinged it good on the lid.

As I stepped back to survey my damage, in my spirit I heard these words, "This is not a spirit of rage. You are in total control of yourself."

I shook off this comment, knocked on the door and told John, "I'm done throwing my fit. Would you please let me in?"

He did, and I proudly showed him how big a dent I had

made in his Weber grill. Of course, he was not in the least impressed with my strength or temper.

No One Left to Blame

I continued to keep my anger in check, never allowing it to embarrass me in public. I reserved it for my home.

I had been raised in a household where you did not attack problems; you attacked people. You searched for someone to blame in order to escape responsibility. I was the one who suffered the majority of physical and emotional abuse and blame as a child. Now I was verbally attacking John whenever I felt helpless or angry.

I did, however, vow to never treat my own children with the anger and abuse I had suffered. My parents were not Christians when they raised me. Once I became a Christian, I believed my conversion would prevent such abuse from reoccurring in my own family.

There was one problem with my reasoning: I had not yet forgiven my mother. It was not because I had forgotten to; I was afraid to forgive her. I thought if I released her she'd be free to hurt me again.

I found myself under intense pressure such as I had never experienced before. My second son had recently been born. My oldest son was two years old and suddenly very uncooperative about going down for afternoon naps. This battle of the naptime had been waging for several weeks. When my newborn was napping, I would put my two-year-old down for a nap in a desperate attempt to do some housework. Each time I left his room and walked down stairs, he jumped off his bed and followed me, arguing that he did not want to take a nap. We went up and down the stairs and back and forth in argument. Finally he would stay down and take a two-hour nap. But as soon as he drifted off to sleep, my newborn would wake up.

One day during just such a struggle I snapped. I grabbed

my two-year-old and stormed upstairs. I thought to myself, *I must make him see that he is not to get off his bed again!* He struggled, kicked and squirmed. I thought, *I need to slam this child against the wall. That will teach him not to get off his bed!* I raised him eye level and was just about to shove him when I saw the fear in his eyes.

At some level he must have sensed I had crossed a threshold in anger that he had not seen before. The terror in his eyes reminded me of my own terror as a child. It was as if in that moment all my childhood fears were masked into his sweet face. This arrested me. I put him down gently on the bed and quietly backed out of his room. I kept repeating, "Mommy is so sorry she scared you." I closed his door and ran downstairs.

I threw myself down on my living room floor and wept until I had no strength left. At that moment I realized the problem did not lie with my parents, my husband, my children, the pressures, my upbringing, my ethnic background, or my hormones — it was with me. Those things were pressures, but I alone was responsible for my reactions to them.

I wept because I doubted I could ever be free from this anger. It had been a part of me for so long that I excused it as a weakness or a personality flaw. Now I had come face-to-face with it. No longer was it draped in excuses. I saw it for what it really was — a destructive self-willed force that I had allowed to control me.

I was alone in that moment with no one to blame. For the first time I felt the entire ugly weight of it on my shoulders. It was as if all the scenes of hateful words and actions were replayed to me, scenes in which I thought I had been justified. Now as I watched them replay in my mind I was horrified by my reactions.

I remembered the Weber grill incident and thought, *I can't go down to the altar for prayer to have this cast out. It is not a spirit.*

Broken, I cried for help, "God I don't want this anymore. I will no longer justify it or blame it on anyone else. Forgive me, Lord." In that moment I felt Him lift the weight of sin and guilt from me. I cried all over again, but this time it was with relief.

When I humbled myself, renounced anger and acknowledged it for what it was, God forgave me and gave me His strength to overcome it.

You Buy What You Justify

> Now the works of the flesh are evident, which are: adultery, fornication, uncleanness, lewdness, idolatry, sorcery, hatred, contentions, jealousies, *outbursts of wrath,* selfish ambitions, dissensions, heresies, envy, murders, drunkenness, revelries and the like (Gal. 5:19-20, NKJV, italics added).

I had bought a lie. This scripture clearly cites outbursts of anger as a product of our earthly, carnal nature. It is not called a spirit or a hereditary tendency or weakness. In Galatians Paul does not make excuses for these. In fact, he goes on to say:

> Those who practice such things will not inherit the kingdom of God (v. 21).

By using the word *practice,* Paul indicates that our actions have become habits. We have sinned the same way so many times that it is now habitual. Don't be quick to make excuses for your flesh. God did not tell us to excuse it, but to crucify it.

> And those who are Christ's have crucified the flesh with its passions and desires (Gal. 5:24, NKJV).

You keep that which you justify. As long as we justify or make excuses we remain captive. By blaming my past I excused my present. I thought the pain of my past earned me the right to behave this way in the present. By blaming others I felt absolved of responsibility. But what about Jesus' past pain? Wasn't it enough to purchase my freedom?

When we refuse to take responsibility, we forfeit our ability to change. *Responsibility* means "the ability to respond." It is our ability to respond that determines our future freedom or lack thereof. When we humble ourselves, admit our iniquity and renounce it, we escape the snare.

Forgive and Forget

After I finished crying, God instructed me to call my mother and ask her forgiveness for all the years I had withheld forgiveness from her. One incident was particularly painful, and I had locked it away in my heart as the grounds for my unforgiveness. I felt prompted by the Spirit to mention that incident to my mother as one of the things included in my forgiveness.

In obedience I called her. Through tears I meekly confessed my sin of unforgiveness, including the incident God had brought to my mind. Then I assured her of my love.

She began to cry. "Lisa, please forgive me for that," she said. "You don't know how the memory of it had weighed upon me." My confession released both of us. My mother is a wonderful woman, and I had allowed a breach to exist between us all those years. Then she prayed a precious prayer for both me and my children. As we prayed together, the power of forgiveness broke the curse over a new generation.

If You're Free Don't Hide It

There is no reason to cover or hide something from

which you have been set free. I was glad that I was free from anger. It was wonderful not to pretend and hide it. I was glad it was over. At the time I had no idea that the private, personal struggles I had hidden would become an integral part of my public testimony.

One day as I prepared to speak at a women's breakfast in Pennsylvania, I asked the Lord, "What do You want me to share today?" I presented a few options I was comfortable with and waited for His leading.

He surprised me. "I want you to get up and tell these women you are a mess."

I was shocked. "God, if I say that, they won't listen. They won't want to hear from a mess!"

"So many of them are in bondage," He replied. "I want you to be open and vulnerable with them. Then they will take down their walls, and I can help them."

Surely I'm not hearing right, I thought. So I asked God again, "What do You want me to minister on?"

He didn't respond.

When I arrived at the breakfast, the women looked me up and down as they measured my worth and ability to speak. I could tell they were assessing my age and appearance. I was very quiet during breakfast. I hoped to hear a new direction from God, but He remained silent.

When the time came to introduce me, the pastor's wife described me in such grand terms I thought she must be introducing someone else. I thought, *Now if I say what God told me she will think I'm being sarcastic.* So I decided I would blame it on God.

I took the mike and told the women, "God told me to tell you I am a mess." They did not know what to do. They were all ready for me to impress them, and now they were disarmed. Some laughed; others just stared blankly with their mouths open.

I shared how God had set me free from anger and

exposed my pride. They began to relax. As they realized I was not going to hurt or intimidate them, they opened their hearts. After the message during the time of ministry, the power of God and word of knowledge flowed freely and unhindered. As soon as the meeting was dismissed, I was swarmed by women who wept and confessed their own bondages. They felt free and safe to do this because I had been open with them.

> Therefore confess your sins to each other and pray for each other so that you may be healed. The prayer of a righteous man is powerful and effective (James 5:16).

That was more than six years ago, and still I am surprised at the number of women who respond when I simply open up and become real and vulnerable with them. Jesus was always real to the people to whom He ministered.

There is power in truth and confession. It is important that we honestly give witness to the power of God that has changed our lives. In doing so we give others encouragement and hope to which they can anchor their faith. It is a chance for them to be courageous and dare to believe God will do the same for them.

> He who conceals his sins does not prosper, but whoever confesses and renounces them finds mercy (Prov. 28:13).

When we are honest we acknowledge His mercy and grace. Openness breaks the hold of shame from your life.

I challenge you to face your anger fearlessly. You may find it lurking in the shadow of excuses. You may have excused it by your past, parents, race or environment, but until you take responsibility for your own actions you will remain a victim of them. You'll be a victim of the destructive havoc your anger rages against you and your loved ones.

God wants to bring you out of the shadows into the light of His liberty. Let these questions penetrate your soul:

- Do you say that others make you angry?

- Do you justify your anger by blaming it on circumstances or pressures around you?

- Do you attack those closest to you?

- Are you afraid of accepting responsibility for your actions?

- Have you accepted anger as a way of life?

By honestly answering these questions, you will accurately assess your position — and sympathy — toward anger. If you have answered yes to any of these, I believe you saw yourself in this chapter. If you are ready to repent and release your anger, God's grace is available even now. From the depth of your heart pray this prayer:

> Father God,
>
> I come before You with brokenness and humility. I have no one left to blame. I bring no excuses. I accept full responsibility for the anger in my life. I lay it at Your feet and humble myself under Your mighty hand of mercy and grace. I receive the power of God imparted into my life. I choose to live free from anger. In the name of Jesus, amen.

The one who gossips to you
gossips of you.

12

Gossip: More Than Mere Words

As a member of a sorority in college I discovered the danger of reentering a room you had just left. Nine times out of ten when you walked back in you'd catch your sorority sisters discussing your vices or virtues. I always took great pains to remember everything I needed before leaving the room. If necessity warranted my return, I tried to make noise in the hall before I opened the door.

It was always painful and embarrassing to hear whispers or laughter suddenly become silent as I walked back in the room for that toothbrush or towel I'd forgotten. I'd scan their faces and know — partly because of the sick feeling in my own stomach — they had just dined on some juicy tidbit.

This was to be expected. In my sorority very few girls claimed to be Christians. I boldly proclaimed myself a heathen committed to the pursuit of pleasure and protection of self! I sought pleasure for the moment and protection from future pain. So I was not above gossiping. I looked at it as self-defense. I mean, women gossip, right?

Then, during the summer between my junior and senior years, to the shock and utter disbelief of all those around me, this heathen became a Christian. Another student on campus led me in the sinner's prayer, and I accepted Jesus as my Lord and Savior. (That young man would later become my husband.) I was gloriously saved, liberated from alcohol and instantly healed of severe lactose intolerance.* It was then that I understood why my shallow, self-centered lifestyle had left me feeling empty.

When I returned to school I found my old surroundings hard to reconcile with my newfound faith. I felt God was leading me to move to Dallas. John, the young man who had shared Christ with me, was there, and I was excited to join a church and be welcomed by my new and true sisters.

Sister Talk

It will be altogether different now! I thought. *The women in church are Christians.* I imagined smiling Christian friends welcoming me with open arms and older women who would disciple me.

Boy, was I in for a shock! They were not the least bit happy to see me. I was not welcomed; instead I was viewed as a competitive threat given the already low population of eligible Christian bachelors.

That first Sunday I felt their disapproval as they sized me from a distance, studying my appearance and demeanor. They were politely cool as I was introduced, then quickly turned the conversation to subjects or persons of which I had no knowledge. For the first time since becoming a

---

*This hereditary disorder caused me to be hospitalized two months earlier due to a severe reaction to a dairy product. After we said a simple prayer, I was able to eat freely pizza, milk shakes and all the other things that had caused me severe pain since my teen years.

Christian I felt strangely awkward.

Judging by the looks I received, I thought it was quite possible they doubted that my conversion was genuine. I had been saved only a few months and had not yet assembled a "sanctified" wardrobe. I owned the wardrobe of a sorority party girl. I had no money to purchase new clothes, so I set about trying to convince them that despite my appearance I was sincere and my intentions honorable. The boys were friendly, but the girls remained distant and distrustful.

Oh well, I thought. *Maybe God doesn't want me to have any girls for friends.*

John had proposed a few months before I arrived in Dallas, but I was not ready to be engaged. All my life I had measured myself by whom I had dated or by my family's social status. Now I wanted to get to know my Father God. I knew God had called me to marry John, but I decided not to date him. I continued school, worked and attended church. I was careful to come to church late, sit alone and leave early. I reasoned that this gave the impression of a fulfilled and busy life. I built a facade to hide how I really lived.

The truth is I was extremely lonely. I had never been alone, and in this solitude I questioned my wisdom in leaving school. I had been starry-eyed and idealistic. It appeared that my sorority contained more warmth, hospitality and compassion than I found in the church. At least I knew what to expect from them. These people totally confused me. I was baffled by this reception from my real sisters.

I spent hours crying to my mother who was a Christian by that time. With my decision to leave the university and attend a Christian college my father stopped covering my expenses. I was alone in a one-room apartment with no friends, furniture or money. I had gone from a rich party girl with lots of friends and social engagements to a poor lonely person living off part-time waitress tips.

One Sunday as I tried to slip out of church unnoticed I

met a young man my age. We laughed and talked for a while, and a few weeks later we went to dinner. About an hour into our meal he blurted out, "You're really not as bad as they say!"

I was astonished. I was certain the reason I had been ignored was because my presence went unnoticed. "As bad as who says?" I questioned.

"Well, you know," he stammered, "all the other girls and my aunt."

My surprise turned to horror! All the other girls and his aunt! She happened to be one of the most influential and prominent women in this five-thousand-member church.

It seemed the women had decided I was conceited. They also were toying with the idea that I had cast a spell of some sort on John so that he would not date anyone. That was why he told everyone he was going to marry me.

Heartbroken, I went home, certain my desire to obey God and leave school was all a mistake. I cried myself to sleep.

Let God Do the Talking

But the next morning at service my sorrow turned to anger as I watched this prominent woman ascend the platform to share something God had laid on her heart. I clenched my fists as I tried to remain composed until she was done.

As soon as church was over, I dashed for my car. Alone with my thoughts, I consoled myself, *I wonder what people would think if they knew what Mrs. High-and-Mighty was really like?*

I was contemplating who and what to tell when I was interrupted by the gentle voice of God. "Lisa, if you defend yourself, I will not defend you."

"But, God, it's not true!" I argued.

"If you start defending yourself now," He answered, "you

will have to do it for the rest of your life." Then He gave me His promise, "If you will not defend yourself, I will be your defense."

I knew my situation was hopeless. Who could I tell anyway? I knew no one in Dallas except those who had maligned me. I was twenty-one years old with no influence, friends or money.

God questioned me, "Lisa, do you know what gossip is?"

I was certain I did, so I answered, "People talking about others irresponsibly."

The Lord gave me a deeper definition. "Gossip is two or more people standing in agreement with the lies of the devil."

"But what if it is true?" I questioned, thinking of what the woman at church did to me. I only wanted to tell the truth about her.

In answer, God described a scenario I could understand. "What if you saw a Christian woman leave a bar on the arm of a man and go home and spend the night with him? What would you think?"

I answered the obvious.

He continued, "Would you be right if you repeated it?"

I felt certain that if I had been an eyewitness and my information was accurate, then it would be all right to repeat it.

"What if she confessed and repented of her sin?" He asked. "What would happen then? What would I do with her iniquity?"

I answered, "You would bury it in the sea of forgetfulness, as far as the east is from the west" (Ps. 103:12).

"Then as far as I would be concerned, it had never happened. If I had forgotten it, then you would have no right to repeat it, would you?"

"No," I answered, "I would have no right."

In this incident God was faithful to defend me. This

woman even took me to lunch eventually and apologized to me herself. But first God had me go to her, humble myself and apologize for acting aloof (remember my feigned busy life). At lunch she confessed she did not know why she had singled me out to gossip about. She said that now she would blow her trumpet just as loudly about what a wonderful young lady I was.

Sweet Nothings

Gossip can be extremely painful. All of us at one time or another have suffered from the wounds of careless words. We have felt the isolation and rejection they bring. We have seen the averted eyes and sensed the distance in others' measured words, words which often carried additional unspoken messages. We have known the turned backs of those who have avoided us.

Perhaps someone with whom you have shared your heart in openness and vulnerability is now closed off to you. You feel as if you were locked out and are not sure why.

All of us can identify with the pain, so why would any of us gossip?

For the most part women are communicators. To some of us, talking is as necessary as eating! Talking is how we sort through information and problems. It is a gift to be able to communicate love, concern, humor and information verbally. It is equally important to use this gift to help others express their deeper feelings and fears. Women are gifted with the ability to surround others with warm words and a supportive atmosphere. This is healthy and necessary. But gossip is not a healthy part of this balanced diet.

Gossip is the Godiva chocolate of conversation. What it lacks in nutritional value it makes up for in taste. Like chocolate, it is tasty, costly and exhilarating for the moment — and void of constructive nutrition. After an initial high you are left with a headache. You know you shouldn't have another morsel, but it tasted so good!

King Solomon described the attraction of gossip this way:

> The words of a talebearer are like tasty trifles, and they go down into the inmost body (Prov. 18:8, NKJV).

These are highly descriptive words. "Tasty trifles" describes something that is delicious and indulgent but minuscule. It is an overdressed little thing — a bit of information or conversation that was assigned too much importance. Unfortunately, this overdressed trivia has the power to penetrate deep into the soul.

The dictionary defines *gossip* as "rumor, defamation, hearsay, scandal, chatter, news, slander." The act of gossiping is described as "to tattle, blab, chatter, noise or tale bear." It is interesting to note that truth is not mentioned anywhere in the definition of gossip. Gossip is a negligent scattering of ungrounded accusations and misrepresentations. It has no credibility or accountability. It is secretive and selective, and its real agenda is always well hidden.

Motives Behind the Methods

I wish I could say I had never gossiped as a Christian, but that would be lying. To my own shame I found out that I could be just as tacky and ugly under pressure as any one else I'd ever seen! Why? Here are my reasons — or excuses. Maybe you will identify with them.

I gossiped to secure or defend myself or a loved one. In other words I gossiped whenever I felt God needed my assistance to protect me or my loved ones. I gossiped to justify or defend myself when I was worried that the other person had not heard my side of the story. I gossiped when I was offended by others. I'd rehearse their flaws or failures because they had hurt me, but I hadn't forgiven them.

Here is an especially interesting reason: I'd gossip to gain someone else's information by bartering mine. It is an unspoken rule that if you take someone into your confidence then they will take you into theirs. This exchange makes both persons vulnerable, which causes both of you to feel somewhat safe. If the other person betrays you, you have something on that person with which to retaliate. This reasoning sounds warped on paper, but nonetheless it is widely practiced.

I was never so calculated as to think through my motives before gossiping. It was only after I allowed God to judge the motives and intents of my heart that I found all these sordid excuses lurking below the surface. One such hidden motive was jealousy.

The Jealousy Factor

We become the prey of jealousy when we mistakenly believe God's favor toward one person indicates His disfavor toward us. Remember Cain? His was the first account of jealousy in the Bible. He perceived Abel's acceptance as his rejection. Unfortunately, even today jealousy is rampant among Christian brethren.

Jealousy breeds competition, which is fueled by gossip. In this arena gossip is not limited to quiet whispers behind someone's back but includes open and public (or even pulpit) slander from others. Those with power and influence will often use it to try to defame those they perceive as threats to their success. Jealousy is a very ugly and consuming fear. There are those who curse their brethren out of jealousy, and it is important to be prepared to respond by blessing them.

Covetousness, desiring what God has given another, is an offspring of jealousy. I never saw myself as someone who would covet until I watched God bless another person with something I needed.

When we first began to travel, we crossed the United States with our three small children packed into a Honda Civic. Every night our family would join hands to pray. In faith we'd thank God for our new van.

In the course of our travels we visited a church where a couple had just been given a van. Though I was happy for them, I was not happy for me! I really needed a van! The couple who received the van attended the church where we ministered. They had fewer children and didn't even travel. God just gave them a van. They were so excited as they shared how God had blessed them. They even admitted they did not really need it.

I thought for certain there had been a mistake. Surely whoever gave it to them was supposed to have given it to me. I knew my reaction was wrong, but I thought, *It is not fair!*

Discouraged, I complained to God about it. My need was greater, so why did He give it to them?

He answered me, "Lisa, you are upset because you see their blessing as a deduction from My ability to bless you. It did not come from your account but Mine. I am unlimited."

Of course God was right. I perceived their blessing as a rejection of my need. Instead of rejoicing with them I had allowed jealousy to turn my focus back to me.

I imagined God's provision as a big storehouse that now contained one less van. I reasoned their blessing had diminished God's ability to supply for me. They had upset my odds of winning!

We are tempted to gossip when we perceive someone else's favor, provision or position as a deduction from God's ability to bless, protect or provide for us.

Drawing Others to Ourselves

Jealousy will even manifest itself in friendships. Perhaps God has blessed us with a friend but we are not certain of the security of this friendship. Because of this we are tempted to discredit anything or anyone we perceive as a threat to this relationship. We malign others to gain the allegiance of our friend. Friendships based on foundations such as this will never last long because soon we become possessive and jealous. We will be offended by the very friend we tried to secure because we perceive any attention our friend gives to another as disloyalty to us.

It is imperative, especially in these times, that we allow God to establish our friendship based on His truth and principles. First make God your best friend.

> He who loves a pure heart and whose speech is gracious will have the king for his friend (Prov. 22:11).

Then let the King choose your friends.

We must desire pure hearts over our needs for friendships. Part of purifying our hearts is refining our speech. Our words are to be gracious or filled with grace. Grace has been described in two different ways:

1. The ability to do what truth demands.

2. Unmerited favor.

Both of these apply to our friendships. To speak graciously requires honoring or covering those who in our estimation don't deserve it. But isn't that what God does for us? He covers us by His blood and honors us with His name. Likewise, we are to cover and honor those around us whether or not we feel they deserve it. God will choose *His* friends for us and thus He will want us to treat them the way He would treat them. Then God will entrust us with true friends because He knows we will be true to them.

Take Heed What You Hear

So far we have discussed gossip in terms of what we say, but gossip is not limited to what is spoken. Often the most difficult and destructive gossip to shake is not what you have said but what you have heard.

> A wicked man listens to evil lips; a liar pays attention to a malicious tongue (Prov. 17:4).

The Bible calls it wicked even to listen to malicious lips. Perhaps you listened to others and thought it was all right because you did not agree with what you heard. You just wanted them to be able to air their grievances to someone safe. Well, it is not safe for them, and it is definitely not safe for you!

As you listened, your own soul was defiled by what you heard. Unknowingly, you now watch for the discussed attributes or character flaws in the accused individual. Amazingly, your eyes are open, and you can see clearly what had been hidden before. You think it is because you are more discerning now. No, it's because you are more suspicious.

Suddenly, whenever you hear that individual's name mentioned, your mind sings the chorus of accusations and complaints you heard earlier. Soon you are wrestling with your own critical thoughts toward that person. You are tempted to judge his or her motives and actions.

This is especially dangerous with leaders and marriage partners.

Listening to gossip about leaders undermines those whom God has placed over us (bosses, parents, teachers or ministers). We become distrustful of the very ones God has put in our lives to guide, provide, train or minister to us.

The gossip we hear is dangerous to our marriage because it cuts off our intimacy. We don't feel free to give ourselves to our partner when we are afraid he may hurt us. It is important when someone comes to you with a complaint about your mate that you make that person aware that you and your mate are one.

In the early years of ministry a few women took me to lunch. One began to tell me how much she liked me, but she felt my husband was too extreme. She cited her reasons and began to criticize John.

I interrupted her. "Please forgive me if I ever gave you the impression that I did not agree with or support John in this position. I do. By speaking against him you are speaking against me. So you can address your complaints to me directly." She immediately stopped. She was more interested in criticizing than in solving anything.

Be careful. Don't allow others, even family members to criticize your mate and undermine your unity. Discern whether they are trying to be constructive or destructive. Often they are unaware of the damaging effect of their words. They think that by pointing out a problem they are giving you answers. Gently correct them.

What Are We to Do?

I have just given a sampling of some gossip pitfalls. I have been open with you so that you will in turn be honest with yourself.

Every time I gossiped I was grieved and vowed never to do it again. This was a constant source of frustration for me. I knew in my heart I did not want to do it, yet it seemed impossible for me to stop. I repented of one scenario only to be caught up in another. It got to the place where I asked God to isolate me until I was able to rise above this pattern or stronghold in my life.

Why had a stronghold been established in my life, and why was it so hard to overcome? Picture an orchard with many rows of fruit trees in your backyard. One row of trees consistently produces bad fruit. The fruit from the trees in this row is diseased and infested with insects and worms. You don't want the pestilence of the bad fruit to spread to your good trees, so weekly you work your way down the row picking off the diseased fruit in order to burn it. But as soon as you've finished the last tree in the row you notice bad fruit has reappeared on the first tree. Frustrated, you start the whole process over.

To accomplish this you must neglect the care of your good trees and their harvest of fruit. The good trees are laden with good fruit, but you are too busy plucking off the bad fruit to harvest it.

To rid yourself of the fruit of gossip you must first destroy the tree. It is useless and frustrating to waste your time destroying the fruit. You need to take an ax to the root that is nourishing the tree and feeding the fruit. These roots are drawing on something that is destroying your fruit.

Gossip is rooted in unbelief and watered by fear. We already know that fear is a spirit and unbelief is a condition of the heart. Therefore we could certainly call gossip a heart condition.

We fall prey to gossip when we are afraid to trust God to uphold us in truth. No matter how complex or unique our situation is, if we are honest we will find fear and unbelief at the root.

We don't forgive because we fear being hurt again. So we stand guard over past offenses. In doing so we prove that we doubt God's ability to heal our past and protect our futures.

We malign others because we believe our worth is tied to theirs. We're afraid if they look good we'll look worse by comparison. This reveals that our self-worth is not founded in Jesus Christ.

We are jealous because we do not believe that God is just. We are afraid He actually plays favorites and honors people instead of faith and obedience. We must remember, anything we receive is by grace and faith in God's goodness.

Healing the Wounds of Gossip

> Reckless words pierce like a sword, but the tongue of the wise brings healing (Prov. 12:18).

Gossip is reckless or careless words that wound. The only way to heal the wounds is to speak words in answer that contain wisdom and promote reconciliation. We are not to answer in the same manner the information was brought to us. An example of such an answer would be to agree with the gossiper and offer our own story about how the offender hurt us too. This would not bring healing. We are instructed:

> Do not answer a fool according to his folly, or you will be like him yourself (Prov. 26:4).

> He who covers over an offense promotes love, but whoever repeats the matter separates close friends (Prov. 17:9).

When we listen to a repeated offense it can separate us from our closest friends. These verses are referring to a hurt or wound from someone close to us. We must develop the wisdom and discernment necessary to answer with words of life. I have found Proverbs to be an excellent source of wisdom to govern my heart. In the appendix of this book is an additional list of scriptures to help you.

It is difficult to safeguard yourself from this type of gossip, but it helps if you ask yourself these questions:

- Why are they telling me this?
- Are they confessing their reaction to the offenses or just repeating it to influence me?
- Have they gone to the individual who offended them?

- Are they asking me to go with them so restoration can take place?

- Am I in a position to help them?

If the answers to these questions are unclear, you are not the one they should be speaking with. They should first speak with the one who offended them.

By studying Proverbs and rehearsing these questions we will not only be able to answer with wisdom, but will also rightly divide our own thoughts and motives. This will carry over when we go to others with our grievances.

Broadsided

Be wary of those things that will weaken your defenses against gossiping. When someone comes to you for counsel, she may intentionally or unknowingly flatter you. This causes you to lose your discernment.

> Do not accept a bribe, for a bribe blinds those who see and twists the words of the righteous (Ex. 23:8).

It is unlikely that someone is going to slip you a twenty-dollar bill. The type of bribe you must guard against is flattery which comes by way of comments such as: "I knew I could bring this to you because you won't tell anyone." This makes us feel trustworthy and as if we are in an exclusive relationship with this person. Under the influence of this type of flattery, I have promised not to repeat matters that would have been better brought into the open. Trustworthiness is proven in time. We can never be certain of the facts until we have heard the whole matter.

Someone may flatter you by saying, "I know you are godly and discerning."

I once received a call from a woman who said she'd heard

I had the ability to interpret dreams. Then she proceeded to tell me not only her dream, but also the interpretation. As a result of her dream she had concluded that her pastor was not a man of the spirit. In actuality she was not asking me anything. She was simply telling me something that she wanted my agreement and support on. Be careful whom you listen to.

When I was a child, there was a precious Irish-Catholic family with eight children who lived around the corner from me. Their mother had decorated her kitchen in a unique way. She had hand-painted assorted proverbs on the walls. I remember one of them distinctly: "He who gossips to you gossips of you."

Experientially, I have found this proverb to be true. Those who carry stories to you, carry stories from you. They will often mention your name by association. "I was at lunch with Lisa the other day. Did you know so-and-so said such and such?" All the other person remembers is your name and the comment. You are now guilty by association.

Speak the Truth

We have to rise up and become people who are willing to be bold enough to see through the flattery of man and speak the truth. By merely listening we validate an offense. We must ask God for the wisdom to speak His restoration and truth. When we attack each other we are warned:

> If you keep on biting and devouring each other, watch out or you will be destroyed by each other (Gal. 5:15).

Why should Satan battle us when he can have us do it for him? Remember, he has been stripped of his weapons. He wants us to be the accuser of the brethren for him. By waging war against each other we fulfill his purpose. It is time to build up, not destroy each other. It is important not to align ourselves with the lies of the enemy, but with the truth of our Father.

What we view as innocent and well-meaning God has a way of revealing for what it really is. When we ask Him to separate the precious from the vile, He points out our hidden flaws and holds them at arm's length to allow us to scrutinize them by His light. His all-revealing light offers a much different perspective than the dim illumination of our intentions does. It is at this point that we see our flaws for what they really are — horrific.

Though we may be tempted to make excuses for our behavior, it is crucial to let the pain and shame of this revelation pierce our hearts at that moment. Then we will turn to our loving Father and ask His forgiveness, renounce our involvement with gossip and rejoice as God hurls it away. If we make the mistake of justifying our behavior we will find ourselves held captive to it.

Ask God to search your heart that you might know the truth and be set free.

Father,

In the name of Jesus, I ask You to open my eyes so that I can rightly divide the motive and intent of my heart. I ask Your forgiveness for each time I have reviled with my words and not trusted You to protect me. I commit myself into Your care. Place a watch over my mouth that I might not sin against You (Ps. 141:3). In Jesus' name, amen.

If allowed, the demands and pressures
around you will always usurp your
priorities and disorder your day.

13

Self-Denial
or Self-Neglect?

---

*E*veryone needs something from me! These words are often uttered through clenched teeth when we feel pulled in every direction. Yet if we are honest, this complaining is accompanied by a sense of self-satisfaction. Things could be worse — what if no one needed us? What if our labor and talent was unnoticed by those around us?

Even in our exasperation we find comfort because we are needed. We sigh and quickly reassure those around us that we can manage our unbearable loads. Why?

Because women need to be needed and men need to be respected. Women are compassionate. It is in our very nature to aid and assist. It is very important that a woman feel indispensable and irreplaceable. To assure this prominence she will often position herself in the lives of her loved ones as the "need-meeter."

But are we the need-meeters? God designed women to

nurture and nurse their husbands, children and loved ones. But what empowers us can become a drain to us if we try to meet all the needs in our own strengths and abilities. Sometimes we are so busy meeting needs that we forget we have needs of our own. Busyness can be our greatest enemy.

Without realizing it women often tend to elevate whatever need is set before them to a position of priority. This is appropriate in the case of emergencies, and it is important to be flexible and spontaneous to a degree. But when the exception becomes a lifestyle it is destructive.

To be effective for Christ we must know what we are to accomplish — the purpose for which we were created? Without priorities in place we will move through our days without purpose, hoping we're going in the right direction.

If allowed, the demands and pressures around us will always usurp our priorities and disorder our days. Soon insignificant crises, interruptions and phone calls have blown us off course. Then activity without purpose navigates our lives. This upheaval wears us out. Our days will be filled with busyness but very little productivity. This drains us and causes us to feel like a failure. This steals our joy, and with it, our strength.

My Frustrating Routine

To explain I want to share some examples from my own life. I often had a hard time accepting help from others. I felt guilty, reasoning that I really should be able to handle it on my own. I thought, *If only I was more organized or got up earlier, I could do it all.* If someone offered to help me, I felt pressured to return the help by entertaining the person or ministering to him or her in some way to appease the guilt of my own inadequacies.

It was easier to do it all myself. But I was constantly distracted and drained of energy. I allowed everyone else's needs to set my priorities.

I spent my days running in circles — responding to this crisis, starting that project, interrupted by another crisis — until I was utterly frustrated and determined just to survive until my children's bedtime when I would get a break.

I'd tuck my last child in around 10 P.M. Then I'd come alive. I could finally accomplish something with the children asleep and the phone quiet. I knew I would not be interrupted. As the rest of the world prepared for bed, I started a load of laundry and headed for the kitchen.

With small boys and a husband who is often gone, I find that my kitchen can be terrifying. I set to work cleaning up the feast of dropped food under the table, then decide I needed to tackle the entire kitchen floor. I have white tile floors and white grout, and keeping it that way is a real challenge. I'd get out the bleach and scouring powder and scrub it with a toothbrush until I felt I was going to pass out from bleach fumes. Then I'd head upstairs to our office to write out checks to pay the bills. It was always between 1 A.M. and 2 A.M. by the time I tumbled into bed.

At 6:30 A.M. the whole cycle started again. I'd stumble into my kitchen to start a coffee IV. My children would watch with a mixture of pity and curiosity. They understood (because I had told them many times) that moms do things for hours while everyone else sleeps.

My oldest son once asked innocently, "Why don't you just go to bed?"

"I can't. Who would do everything?" I explained.

"Oh," he nodded sadly.

I'd listen to my children's bedtime prayers, and my second son prayed regularly, "God, let Mommy be fresh in the morning." But I never was.

So they'd watch helplessly as I'd wander the kitchen from counter to counter like a pinball, trying to pack lunch and make breakfast. I'd rush my oldest son off to school, clean up the kitchen and attempt to get in the shower before the phone started ringing — but I'd never quite make it. It was 9 A.M. and the rest of the world was already awake and showered.

I'd become frustrated with the interruptions, usually getting out of the shower just in time to start lunch. After lunch I'd only get an hour's worth of work done before it was time to pick up the kids from school.

Such was my daily cycle.

While pregnant with my fourth son I became anemic. My husband put his foot down. He made me hire a cleaning lady to come in twice a month. It helped, but during the other two weeks in the month the messes would not wait.

One night when I was four months pregnant, I was down on my hands and knees scrubbing my tile floor at midnight. I proudly gloated to myself, *No cleaning lady gets my floor this clean. No one gets this grout as white as I do.*

God interrupted me, "Lisa, when you stand before Me I am not going to reward you because you cleaned your own tile floor the best. You'll be rewarded by how faithful you were with what I told you to do. Let all this little stuff go." Suddenly my boasting seemed so stupid, my exhaustion so useless. I already knew what would happen the next morning. I would wake up tired and grumpy, running behind before my day even began.

But I was stubborn. I received my self-worth by doing all these things. I enjoyed being viewed as a martyr by my family. I reasoned, *I'll just get up at 6 A.M. and take my shower before my children are up so I can be more organized. Then I can continue doing all my housework, the administration of the ministry and care for the children.* So I continued to do everything and still found myself running behind.

I was deriving my self-worth from something other than God. I derived it from my selfless labor for my family. But, in fact, I was not selfless. I was selfish to withhold from them what really mattered — my time and attention.

Neglecting Self and Family

In the fifth month of my pregnancy my car was hit from behind. The baby was fine, but now I was pregnant and suffering from whiplash. I was no longer physically able to do all the busy stuff. I had to face my physical limitations and distorted perceptions. Finally I threw up my hands and hired a cleaning lady to come every week until I had the baby.

Why did I wait until I was totally incapacitated before I gave up? Because I was busy and troubled with many things. I had confused self-denial with self-neglect. I thought by caring for everyone but me I was denying myself. It made me feel needed and spiritual. But in truth I was denying my family; I was denying God's call on my life; and I was neglecting myself.

Self-denial is laying down our natural will to choose to pursue God's purpose.

> Then Jesus said to his disciples, "If anyone would come after me, he must deny himself and take up his cross and follow me" (Matt. 16:24).

I denied my children a rested, pleasantly awake mother in the morning. I denied my husband and children quality time with me because I was always tense and distracted. I felt the need to labor endlessly because I was under the constant weight of all I had yet to finish.

When my husband was home I denied him a wife in bed with him because of my wacky schedule. I stayed up much later than he did or sneaked out of the room once he was asleep. I denied my children access to me. Unintentionally, I pushed them aside when I allowed every phone call to interrupt our time together. Then I rushed them off to bed. I was not enjoying my husband and children — I was surviving them!

Martha Mom

I had become a Martha mom. I deprived myself of sleep, exercise and recreation. I neglected the joy of my marriage and children. For what reason? To take care of "things."

Worst of all I neglected myself spiritually, always giving out and never taking in. This neglect was not for spiritual gain but for mommy busyness. I was such a Martha! I'd get down on the floor to pray and notice a Lego under the sofa. After putting it away I discovered something else amiss. Soon I was cleaning the entire upstairs, totally forgetting I had kneeled down to pray.

> "Martha, Martha," the Lord answered, "you are worried and upset about many things, but only one thing is needed. Mary has chosen what is better, and it will not be taken away from her" (Luke 10:41-42).

Sometimes we just have to let the Legos lie, close our eyes, tune out all that would distract us and press in to God. At first this may seem more difficult than cleaning. We are used to activity. That's how we feel needed. Martha wanted Mary in the kitchen laboring over the food preparation. Mary had the attitude, "I can eat later; right now Jesus is talking, and I want to hear Him." Our time of prayer, praise or worship is not another demand the Lord places on us. It is something He provides for our refreshing.

I used to view prayer as just one more thing I had not accomplished at the end of my day. I did pray every day, but I wanted to have two full hours in the closet (which I'm sure I would have begun to straighten). At the end of the day when I was finally able to squeeze in a few minutes with God, I thought He was upset because I hadn't given Him two hours earlier, so I would spend my prayer time apologizing. One day He interrupted my condemnation report. "This is for you!" He said. "Stop seeing Me as angry at you for not coming earlier. I am glad we are together now. Let Me refresh you so you will look forward to these times together." This revolutionized my outlook on prayer.

When we busy ourselves with the temporary to the neglect of the eternal, we become frustrated. We blame those around us even though our frustration is due to a lack of our own refreshing. We are not refreshed because we are too busy taking care of everything so others can be refreshed. Then we get mad at them when they are not running at our hectic pace, and we are still frantically banging pots and pans in the kitchen. We need to throw down our pots and pans and enjoy God and each other.

God showed me that I could experience the same refreshing I received in His presence as I spent time with my husband and children. I had become too busy being a mother to be a nurturer. Too busy being a wife to be a companion. After all, I felt I proved my love by meeting needs.

When John asked me to go golfing with him, I replied, "I don't have time to golf!" I was irritated that he did.

The truth was I had time for what I made time for. But I had not allotted any time for recreation or enjoyment. I was so driven to care for the ones I loved that I had forgotten to enjoy them.

Remember, God made us for companionship. He gave the woman to the man so the man would not be alone. He wanted them to enjoy each other and all that He had created for them. When we replace our time of fellowship with Him with the works of our hands we are spent of our strength.

The same is true of children and friends. If we do not spend time developing these relationships they will eventually quit growing.

How can we safeguard our time from this theft? How can we keep our perspective correct? What should our priorities be? I know there are already many good books on how to order your day, time and priorities. One advises this order: God, husband, children, job, church, yourself. Another recommends: God, yourself, ministry, husband, children, church, job, friends. I'm not going to attempt to compile a list for fear it would be used as a formula.

I don't believe a formula exists! If it did, it certainly would not be found within my wisdom. The longer I walk with God, the more I realize that formulas, rules and laws lead inevitably to the path of religion. Just ask yourself, What is my motive?

What Are You Laboring For?

You can never correctly order your priorities until they've been assigned value and worth. I'm not referring to *time management* as much as I am to *heart management*.

The children of Israel wanted a list of rules and formulas more than a relationship with their Creator. They had every possible detail spelled out for them on how to obey God and stay holy. But it didn't work.

Jesus summed it up this way:

> Love the Lord your God with all your heart and with all your soul and with all your mind...Love your neighbor as yourself (Matt. 22:37-38).

He took away lifeless, rigid structure. He did not tell them how to love God and their neighbors. Jesus knew that if their hearts were pure, then their actions would follow.

What is our value structure? Can we be trusted to create one? No, because our very nature is to be busy and distracted, not only at home but at church and at our jobs. We cannot trust ourselves to measure accurately the merit of what God has placed in our care.

We live in a world whose standard is relative. It drifts on a sea of uncertainty and constant change. This standard shifts and slides with the rise and fall of each wave. Good is bad, and bad is good. This floating morality does not value or esteem what God esteems. Our culture rewards achievement and appearance, but God rewards faithfulness and substance.

Things Are Not What They Seem

Unfortunately, many a Christian is busy laboring to appear to be someone of substance and accomplishment. This leaves the person feeling void and fearful. Appearances are very laborious to maintain. Any strength they yield is expended in their constant protection. Appearances drain us of the energy we need to change.

Appearance by definition means "presentation, air, bearing, semblance, or demeanor." In contrast, *substance* is defined as "the essence, matter, element or material." This definition suggests the very life or truth of an issue, person or thing. What it is made of, not merely what it is cloaked in.

The truth is not ashamed; it is open and rides the winds of principles that supersede time. Appearances merely cover over the outward and gain their strength through deception. Time is the captor of appearance, and ultimately time exposes and destroys it. God's ways are higher than our own. His truth and principles live on. The truth always outlives a lie.

I challenge you to examine your lifestyle honestly. Are you so busy you neglect yourself and those you love? Have you mistaken self-neglect for self-denial? What are you laboring for? Are you drawing your security from the little things or have you focused on the eternal?

If your answer to any of these questions is yes, don't use them as an excuse for a guilt trip. Instead, let them motivate you to change.

PART III

Free at Last

The river of God will take us places
we've never been in a manner
we're unaccustomed to.

14

Over Your Head
and Out of Control

When I was five I was fearless, especially around water. The only way my parents could convince me to take swimming lessons was to forbid me from going off the high dive unless I took them. Even though I was unable to swim, I would scale the ten-foot board, encircled by my inner tube, and plunge feet first into the water whenever the lifeguard was not watching.

As soon as I took swimming lessons I excelled, and soon I was swimming competitively year round. I started in the six-year-old-and-under category and swam competitively until college.

I grew up in Indiana, and our family took yearly spring vacations to Florida. It was there I developed a love for body surfing. I spent my entire day at the beach. The bigger the waves, the better. I would wade out and position myself to wait for that precise moment when, if I swam fast enough, I could match the momentum of the wave. When I caught it, it lifted me and carried me to the shore. Upon arrival I was tossed head over heels into the shallow water while the wave spent its strength on the beach.

I would struggle to my feet among the swirling sand and water and yell to my mom and anyone else who cared to listen, "Hey, did you see how far I went that time?"

Again I waded out, diving through the middle of the oncoming waves. I waited again until I found another wave to carry me in. I had no fear of the waves or water. I enjoyed exchanging my control and contact with the ocean floor for the exhilaration of the wave's ride.

As I got older I was not so free. I became self-conscious. I noticed others as they watched me, and I wondered how I looked to them. Perhaps I looked awkward tumbling in to the shore. Then there was the matter of the bothersome sand in my suit and the issue of modesty as my top would come up or my bottoms would fall down. The fears of how I looked to the nameless observers on the beach robbed my joy of swimming.

I thought, *I'm grown up and mature. Who needs the messy sand or turbulent ocean?* I wanted nothing more aggressive than a pool. In a pool I could get refreshed, but I could also determine when, where, how deep and how often I wanted to go.

It wasn't long before I felt that it was a bother to get wet — period. It messed up my hair and makeup. It was too cold! I lost all my enjoyment of water. If I did venture in water, I found myself apprehensive and timid if I was not in a pool.

It's Not My Element

Swimming affords us a unique opportunity to experience an element and environment we do not normally live in. It gives us the chance to play in something that has the potential to kill us. Water is to be respected. It does not play by our rules; we must play by its rules. We cannot live without water, but we cannot live in it, either.

I can hear some of you saying, "I don't like swimming." But what is it about swimming that you do not like?

Is it the temperature? Are you afraid when you can't touch or see the bottom? Are you afraid of what is under the water? Is it still and deep water that frightens you or shallow and turbulent water? Is it depth or waves? Is it because you cannot breathe under water? Do you feel uncovered in a bathing suit? Perhaps you cannot swim.

I decided I had enough swimming. It was time for my children to enjoy it as I watched from the shore. But the Spirit whispered this reminder to me:

"You love to swim."

"No, I don't," I argued.

"You like it over your head. You like the deep end."

"Not anymore." I countered.

You see, now I was dealing with more than just the uncomfortable or undignified. I had become afraid — not just of water but of anything that possessed the power or the strength to sweep me off my feet and go over my head.

I was in a time of change and transition. I wanted the assurance of what to expect ahead of time. I wanted to plan. I did not want any more surprises. I was older now. I knew my limitations and levels of comfort and did not want them violated. In order to maintain this position I had drawn back to protect myself. If I took too many steps forward, I would venture into the domain of the unsure and unexpected. So I paced the shore of indecision with a wary eye on the water.

It Is Time to Go Swimming

But the shore teemed with fears of its own. Fear of failure, fear of error, fear of staying ashore, fear of leaving it. Fear,

fear, fear — it seemed to immobilize me more than anything else in my life.

I was becoming irritated by the limits I had set to protect myself. My restlessness occurred in conjunction with a release in my life that came as I read Isaiah 52:1-2. God was awakening my interest in adventure. It seemed He wanted me free from my bondage so I could turn total control over to Him. No sooner did I throw off my chains than He told me to jump into water that was over my head.

For the first time I noticed fear speaking into my mind. I would think, *Now, where did that come from?* I knew it was important to resist fear to remain free, but I wasn't sure about relinquishing the small amount of control over my life I now enjoyed. Then God showed me His river and whispered His prompting encouragement, "Remember, you like to swim."

The River of God

I found this river in Ezekiel. It is the river that issues forth from the threshold of the temple of God and the throne room of His prince (Ezek. 47:1-2).

By means of a vision, Ezekiel was brought back to Jerusalem from exile. He stood in the temple where he was given very specific details and directives for temple service and worship practices. He was accompanied by "a man whose appearance was like bronze; he was standing in the gateway with a linen cord and a measuring rod in his hand" (Ezek. 40:3).

They recorded every measurement and ordinance of worship. This man showed Ezekiel the glory of the Lord at the eastern gate. Then Ezekiel was lifted by the Spirit into the inner court where he watched as the glory of the Lord filled the temple.

In chapter 47 Ezekiel was brought outside the temple to a river that flowed from the south side of the temple. It was much more than a natural river; it was the river of God's glory proceeding forth from His throne.

The man of bronze brought Ezekiel to the bank of the river of God and measured it off at thousand-cubit intervals from the shore. At each interval he led Ezekiel out into the water so he could experience the depth of the river at that particular distance from shore.

> As the man went eastward with a measuring line in his hand, he measured off a thousand cubits and then led me through water that was ankle-deep (Ezek. 47:3).

At the first thousand cubits it was only ankle deep. In water this shallow you can walk around freely. You can still see the bottom so you know whether it is sand or rock that you walk upon. The ground is holding you up. You're in the water, but you're still on land. You can quickly splash through ankle-deep water with little or no resistance from the water. You can feel its coolness and be refreshed, but whenever you want you can turn and walk back to shore.

> He measured off another thousand cubits and led me through water that was knee-deep (Ezek. 47:4).

Knee-deep water can begin to slow down your progress some. Depending on the strength of the current you may have trouble walking a straight line unless you have something to align yourself with on the shore.

If you don't maintain your position with a reference point, you will always find that the current has carried you downstream. Knee-deep water will have more influence on you than ankle-deep water. If you try to move too swiftly through it, you will lose your footing and find yourself wet. But in this depth it is easy to stand to your feet again, turn and retrace your way back to the shore.

> He measured off another thousand and led me
> through water that was up to the waist (Ezek.
> 47:4).

Waist-deep water is another story. Now you are half in and half out of the water. Your progress through the water is much more laborious. More than likely you have lost sight of the bottom of the river. You know it is there only because you feel it underfoot. But feeling something you cannot see is not as comfortable as seeing what you cannot feel. The waters have a lot of influence on your progress and direction now. Waist-deep water is usually easier to swim in than walk through, but because the bottom is no longer visible, it's hard to give up your contact with it.

> He measured off another thousand, but now it
> was a river that I could not cross, because the
> water had risen and was deep enough to swim in
> — a river that no one could cross. He asked me,
> "Son of man, do you see this?" (Ezek. 47:5-6).

Now the water was over Ezekiel's head. He could not see the bottom of the river nor did he have any contact with it. He was no longer held upright by the solid river bottom; he was now held up by the river. He was under its control. Ezekiel was totally surrounded by an element he could not walk in or breathe. He was propelled by its fast-moving, powerful currents. All progress was dictated by the river's flow. The current determined his speed and distance.

You have no influence on this type of river, but it certainly has influence on you. Ezekiel described it as deep enough for swimming but impossible to cross. If you fought against the current, at best you would be exhausted. You could drown. Your best chance is to yield to the river and travel where it leads you.

The river of God will surround, uphold, carry, transport,

refresh and at times overwhelm you. Everywhere this river flows it brings life.

> Swarms of living creatures will live wherever the river flows. There will be large numbers of fish, because this water flows there and makes the salt water fresh; so where the river flows everything will live...Fruit trees of all kinds will grow on both banks of the river. Their leaves will not wither, nor will their fruit fail. Every month they will bear, because the water from the sanctuary flows to them. Their fruit will serve for food and their leaves for healing (Ezek. 47:9,12).

It is a river of vibrant life that brings life everywhere it flows. But we are warned not to cross it. When God flows by His Spirit we cannot cross Him. He wanted to be certain that Ezekiel saw clearly and experienced the strength and magnitude of this river.

Don't Cross the Holy Spirit

What does it mean to cross something? When we oppose, contradict, frustrate or are cynical about the flow of God's Spirit, we cross Him. We also cross the Spirit of God when we mix what He is doing with something He is not. This could mean mixing the glory of man with the glory of God. It could mean that we merchandised the flow of God. It could mean a zeal without knowledge.

Look how Jesus confronted Paul when he crossed the early church by persecuting it.

> He fell to the ground and heard a voice say to him, "Saul, Saul, why do you persecute me?" "Who are you, Lord?" Saul asked. "I am Jesus, whom you are persecuting," he replied (Acts 9:4-5).

Jesus did not say, "Hey, Saul, stop hurting My church!" He accused Saul of persecuting Him. Not once, but twice He expressed this. I'm sure Saul (Paul) was surprised. He thought he was on a mission from God. He knew the names of those he had imprisoned or executed, but who was this?

Peter also recognized the importance of not crossing the Holy Spirit. He had just preached to the gentiles, and they had been gloriously baptized in the Holy Ghost. When Peter returned to Jerusalem, the leaders of the church rebuked him for ministering to gentiles. Peter explained to them what had happened:

> As I began to speak, the Holy Spirit came on them as he had come on us at the beginning. Then I remembered what the Lord had said: "John baptized with water, but you will be baptized with the Holy Spirit." So if God gave them the same gift as he gave us, who believed in the Lord Jesus Christ, who was I to think that I could oppose God?
>
> When they heard this, they had no further objections and praised God, saying, "So then, God has granted even the Gentiles repentance unto life" (Acts 11:15-18).

Peter knew better than to try to control something God was doing. He understood that he should not cross God. A holy fear and reverence overshadowed all that the Spirit was doing. The leaders yielded even though it contradicted Jewish law and tradition.

God's river will flow independently of the approval of man. It will not be supplied by man because it originated from the very threshold of the throne of God. Nor will it be altered by man. The river's course is set by the Spirit, not by our agendas. It will take us places we've never been in a manner we're unaccustomed to.

Did you notice the entrance to the river is graduated?

You do not start out over your head. It starts out ankle deep, then it progresses to the knee, then it rises to the waist. This allows us to adjust to the temperature and current. Then the ground suddenly drops off and the water covers our heads. This is the point at which we must surrender all our control to the current. This is when we let go and allow God to exercise His control over our care, course and destination.

Beachcombers

In the spirit people are mulling on the shores of decision. Do they wade in and test the water? Should they wander in to their waist or take the plunge and totally relinquish control to the river?

Some of you desperately long to leap with abandon into the current of this river. If you could, you would be in over your head in a moment's time, but something holds you back.

You are entangled. People are pleading with you from the beach, "Don't go out any farther. I need you! Don't leave me behind! Just stay a little longer!" Your heart is drawn by the water, but you feel compelled to stay with those on the shore.

I know this sounds hard, but you must turn from their pleas and embrace the water. It is the only way you will ever truly be able to help them. The voices are usually those of family members. Jesus told us we would face this time of separation:

> If anyone comes to me and does not hate his father and mother, his wife and children, his brothers and sisters — yes, even his own life — he cannot be my disciple (Luke 14:26).

The Amplified Bible explains the word "hate" as "the

sense of indifference or relative disregard for them [family] in comparison with our attitude toward God." Jesus is exposing any tie that would bind us to something other than Him.

Separated by the Sword

In my own life I have heard those voices on the shore. There was one in particular I felt compelled to listen to. I felt so responsible for this loved one that it had become unhealthy.

If this person was not happy and I was, I felt guilty. If this person had a problem, it became mine. I mediated this person's relations with the rest of the family. I was weighed down as I tried to solve this one's problems. If my solution did not work, I felt responsible. I was so entangled that this person's very mood swings affected my life and marriage. No one, not even my husband, had this effect on me.

For years I wrestled with this relationship. I knew it was unhealthy, but I just could not seem to break away from it. I wanted to show my love and respect to this person, but the control I felt made it difficult. I opened up to a friend who shared these words of Jesus with me.

> Do not suppose that I have come to bring peace to the earth. I did not come to bring peace, but a sword. For I have come to turn a man against his father, a daughter against her mother, a daughter-in-law against her mother-in-law (Matt. 10:34-35).

This scripture seemed too harsh. This person was a Christian. What would be the reason to turn against this one? I did not want to be alienated. I just wanted things to be healthy.

I read it again. This time as I read it, I saw an angel in my mind's eye. Upright in his hand he held a sword of light. I heard the Lord say, "Let Me pass My sword between the two of you."

I could tell the angel was waiting for my permission. He would do nothing unless I instructed him. The Lord continued, "Lisa, you see this sword as an instrument of destruction. My sword has two edges. With one side it severs and with the other it heals." Then He gave me this familiar scripture:

> For the word of God is living and active. Sharper than any double-edged sword, it penetrates even to dividing soul and spirit, joints and marrow; it judges the thoughts and attitudes of the heart (Heb. 4:12).

I thought more about the relationship in question. I saw that I had a deep-rooted need for this person's approval. I had contributed an unhealthy portion to this relationship by trying to meet needs only Jesus could meet. Is it any wonder I was doomed to frustration?

I knew Jesus was asking me to allow Him to do what I could not.

He was not going to name and identify each cord that had bound us. He was going to cut them! My behavior had bound both of us. When I saw this, I closed my eyes and asked God by His Spirit to cut us free. I watched as the saber of light passed between us in an instant.

Immediately I felt that I owed this person nothing but my love. Some aspects did not change overnight, but they did change. Now this relationship is healthy and sound.

Many of you need to allow the Word of God to pass between you and any entanglements that hold you back. Obey the Lord and answer the Spirit's call to relinquish your control.

Release into His care your husband, loved ones, friends,

worries, fears and, most of all, yourself. You will experience a freedom such as you have never known by simply letting go.

If you are ready, say this prayer:

> Father,
>
> I come before You and ask Your forgiveness for allowing others to hold me back. Forgive me for trying to take a place in their lives that only You can fill. Lord, pass Your sword between _____ and myself. Let nothing stand between us but You. I release this person into Your care and surrender myself to Your flow and direction for my life. Overflow me by Your Spirit and wash me in Your flood.

Let the river of God overflow and overtake you. The river will bring life to all those you love. How can you refresh others when you are not refreshed? So wade out and take the plunge.

Epilogue

B ut for you who revere my name, the sun of right-eousness will rise with healing in its wings. And you will go out and leap like calves released from the stall" (Mal. 4:2).

Have you ever seen a calf released from its stall? As soon as the door is opened it bolts, leaping, kicking, bounding and stretching. Watching this, you begin to wonder how the stall ever contained it!

God used this analogy to describe the release of His own people, those who revere and honor His name. They had been pinned up in a stall. Now He wants them free to feed and frolic in the fields.

Notice that before He frees them He is going to heal them. His sun of righteousness will arise with healing. The sun is a ball of constant and consuming fire. We can be certain God is speaking about fire for in Malachi 4:1 it says:

"Surely the day is coming; it will burn like a furnace. All the arrogant and every evildoer will be stubble, and that day that is coming will set them on fire," says the Lord Almighty. "Not a root or a branch will be left to them."

This describes the refining fire of God's judgment on the proud and wicked. It will burn them until there is nothing left. The same fire that destroys them will purify and heal the believers who love and fear God. The Word of God gives light and life to us, but the same Word pronounces judgment on the world of unbelievers.

After God heals and releases us, we will "trample down the wicked; they will be ashes under the soles of your feet on the day when I do these things" (Mal. 4:3). Are you ready to be released?

In this book I have shared candidly in the hope that through my openness you might glimpse yourself. It is my prayer that by freely sharing my bondage you can identify with Christ's process of liberation. I have written this from my heart to yours.

Something higher awaits you, a freedom like none you've ever known. It is a priceless freedom that you must fight to maintain. Yet you must allow God to be the One to judge those around you. You need only to submit to God's refining and healing process.

I believe the truths in this book are part of that process. You will know the truth, and it will set you free. It will release you from all captivity.

Now it is time to trample and tread underfoot every yoke of bondage and weight that the enemy has laid upon your shoulders. Throw off the yoke of control. Give God the care of everything. Release it all.

I want you to envision any care or hindrance that weighs you down as that yoke of bondage. Lift it off your shoulders and throw it at your feet. Write down your cares on a sheet of paper and place it on the floor. Now address it in prayer:

> Control and fear, I address you in the name of Jesus. I refuse to be under your bondage or servitude. I renounce your burden. I will take no yoke of religion or fear of man. I am only yoked alongside my Master, Jesus Christ. I relinquish control of my life, family, friends, finances, security and position. I trample you under my feet to signify that the fire of God has broken your hold from my life.

Thanks be to God who gives us the victory!

APPENDIX

Proverbs Related to Gossip

The wise in heart are called discerning, and pleasant words promote instruction (16:21).

With his mouth the godless destroys his neighbor, but through knowledge the righteous escape (11:9).

The words of the wicked lie in wait for blood, but the speech of the upright rescues them (12:6).

The discerning heart seeks knowledge, but the mouth of a fool feeds on folly (15:14).

The heart of the righteous weighs its answers, but the mouth of the wicked gushes evil (15:28).

A wise man's heart guides his mouth, and his lips promote instruction. Pleasant words are a honeycomb, sweet to the soul and healing to the bones (16:23-24).

A man's wisdom gives him patience; it is to his glory to overlook an offense (19:11).

It is to a man's honor to avoid strife, but every fool is quick to quarrel (20:3).

Without wood a fire goes out; without gossip a quarrel dies down (26:20).

He who conceals his sins does not prosper, but whoever confesses and renounces them finds mercy (28:13).

To receive JBM's newsletter, *The Messenger,* and a free catalog of ministry resources, please contact us at:

John Bevere Ministries
World Headquarters
P. O. Box 888
Palmer Lake, CO 80133-0888
Tel: 800-648-1477 (inside the U.S.)
Tel: 719-487-3000
Fax: 719-487-3300
E-mail: jbm@johnbevere.org
Website: www.johnbevere.org

Europe and Africa
P. O. Box 2794
Walsall
WS2 7YQ
UNITED KINGDOM
Tel: 44-0870-745-5790
Fax: 44-0870-745-5791

The Messenger television program airs on
The Christian Channel Europe.
Please check your local listings for day and time.

Australia
P .O. Box 6200
Dural D.C. NSW 2158
AUSTRALIA
Tel: 61-02-8850-1725

OTHER BOOKS by John and Lisa Bevere

Thus Saith the Lord? by John Bevere

You can discern truth from deception. Jesus sternly warned, "See to it that no one misleads you" (Matt. 24:4, NAS). To be misled is to be deceived. Jesus makes it clear—it is our responsiblity to discern truth from deception. This includes rightly dividing genuine spiritual authority from counterfeit. This book reveals how to recognize true and false authority and the deceptive tactics of false authority.

The Fear of the Lord by John Bevere

There's something missing in our churches, our prayers and in our personal lives. It's what builds intimacy in our relationship with God, makes our lives real and pure and transforms us into truly Spirit-led children of God. It is the fear of the Lord. This book challenges us to fear God and reverence Him anew in our worship and daily lives.

The Bait of Satan by John Bevere

This book exposes one of the most deceptive snares that Satan uses to get believers out of the will of God—the trap of offense. Most who are ensnared do not even realize it. But everyone must be made aware of this trap, because Jesus said, "It is impossible that offenses will not come" (Luke 17:1). The question is not, "Will you encounter the bait of Satan?" Rather, it is, "How will you respond?" *Your response determines your future!*

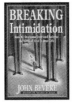

Breaking Intimidation by John Bevere

Countless Christians battle intimidation. The Bible is filled with examples of God's people facing intimidation. Some overcame while others were overcome. This book is an in-depth look at these ancient references and present-day scenarios. The goal: to expose intimidation, break its fearful grip and release God's gift and dominion in your life.

Victory in the Wilderness by John Bevere

Does it seem your spiritual progress in the Lord has come to a halt—or even regressed? You wonder if you have missed God or somehow displeased Him, but that is not the case. You've just arrived at the wilderness! The wilderness is not God's rejection, but the season of preparation in your life. God intends for you to have *Victory in the Wilderness.*

The Voice of One Crying by John Bevere

God is restoring the prophetic to turn the hearts of His people to Him. Yet this office is often reduced to one who predicts the future by a word of knowledge or wisdom...rather than a declaration of the church's true condition and destiny. Many, fed up with hype and superficial ministry, are ready to receive the true prophetic message.

You Are Not What You Weigh by Lisa Bevere

Are you tired of reading trendy diet books, taking faddish pills and ordering the latest in television infomercial exercise equipment? Break free from the destructive cycle of dieting and apprehend true freedom. Discover riveting truths from God's Word with the power to set you free. Trade your *self* consciousness for a deeper consciousness of God.

The True Measure of a Woman by Lisa Bevere

A woman often measures herself and her own worth according to the standards set by others around her. Her self-esteem rises and falls with the whims of popular opinion as she allows other people to control how she thinks about herself. This interactive book will help you unveil the truth of God's Word—truth that will displace any lies and help you discover who you are in Christ.

Out of Control and Loving It! by Lisa Bevere

Is your life a whirlwind of turmoil? Are you tired of pretending to be free only to remain captive? It is because you are in control! In this candid and honest book, Lisa challenges you to relinquish control of your life to God and abandon yourself to His care.

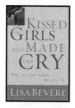

Kissed the Girls and Made Them Cry by Lisa Bevere

Women were created for so much more than being a sexual outlet for men. It is time to restore dignity, honor, strength and power to generations of women, young and old, who are no longer willing to lose.

Under Cover by John Bevere

Under Cover exposes the subtle yet rampant tactics the enemy uses against believers—the failure to recognize and properly relate to divine authority. With practical, personal examples and stern, biblical foundation, this book reminds us the kingdom of God is just that—a kingdom, ruled by a King, where there is order and authority.